THE BOOK OF BORN FREE

THE WISDOM
OF
LIVING RIGHT NOW!

Volume One

Born Free

THE BOOK OF BORN FREE

THE WISDOM
OF
LIVING RIGHT NOW!

Volume One

Born Free

Conscious Commentary Publishing LLC

The Book of Born Free - Volume One

**Carl Born Free Wharton
The Book of Born Free
The Wisdom of Living Right Now!
Volume One**

All right's reserved. Printed in the United States of America. No part of this book can be reproduced in any written, electronic, digital, recording, or photocopying form without the explicit permission by the author or the publisher. The only exception is in the case of reprints in the context of reviews.

**Front and Back covers created by
Safiya Wharton of QVision
follow on IG and Fiverr @
https://www.instagram.com/qvision223
https://www.fiverr.com/qvision223**

Graphic design by Wallace Ford and Aremjndi –

ISBN-13: 978-0692904619
ISBN-10: 0692904611

Follow on all social media platforms #therealbornfree

Copyright © 2017 **Conscious Commentary Publishing LLC**

The Book of Born Free - Volume One

Controlling the food supply
Choosing who should live or die
Confusion rules you choose the lie
Illusion illuminates your mind
These are the last times
Spend time getting organized
Victory be with the strongest tribe
The ones that forge the tightest ties"

Wise Intelligent

"And now these three remain:
faith, hope and love
But the greatest of these is love"

1 Corinthians 13:13

"always love the God
of Abraham, Isaac, and Jacob.
never forget that you are a child of the Creator.
you were born to be great
and never believe a damn word that Esau says!
he's a liar!"

Pauline Ramsey

The Book of Born Free - Volume One

The Ingredients:

Acknowledgements

My Opening Statement

Introduction by
**Wise Intelligent
(Poor Righteous Teachers)**

*My Unapologetic Black Perspective and the
Political Ramifications of Living Right Now!*
(Jewels #1-360) – page 1 to 141

*My Loving Black Erotica and my Delicious
Desire for Living Right Now*
(Jewels #361-630) – page 142 to 251

The Book of Born Free - Volume One

ACKNOWLEDGEMENTS

First, all glory and praises go to the Most High God of Abraham, Isaac, Jacob, Sarah, Rebecca, Rachel, and Leah. I am a child of The Infinite & Eternal YHWH, Adonai, Jehovah, YAH, The Creator, Elohim, The Universal Life Force, The Alpha and The Omega, Ogun & Oshun, Yemaya, Shango, Allah, The Creative Principle, The Christ Consciousness, Jesus, God, The Divine & Supreme Mind, The Supreme Father & The Supreme Mother, Nature, The True Self, The Pure & True Love, The Gaia, Ma'at, The Lord of All the Worlds, and The All in All. I exist because YOU exist. Your purpose is my purpose. Your laws are my laws. Your life is my life. Thank you for allowing me to love, look, listen, learn, understand, and to feel. Without YOU as my foundation I could never stand up to help motivate our youth towards positive attitudes and lifestyles.

This book is dedicated to my Beloved Grandmother Pauline Ramsey my first Hebrew Queen, who taught and commanded us to always obey the God of Abraham, Isaac, and Jacob, Sarah, Rebecca, Rachel, and Leah. She taught us the Shema Israel ("Hear, O Israel The LORD our God, the LORD is one" Deuteronomy 6:4) and showed us how to live a loving life of dignity, faith, courage, service, and high purpose. I also dedicate this book to my Beloved daughter Safiya, who's my supreme gift from the Creator and the greatest manifestation of God's infinite love and grace that I've ever experienced. Thanks for allowing me to showcase your incredible art. You captured exactly what I wanted to express. You painted the perfect scenes on the front and back cover. Your vision is brilliant! Your talent continues to inspire me. I can't wait until we open our comic book store!!! It's going to be-crazy fun! #buddypals4life

Complete love and respect go to my parents, Roland and Hattie Wharton. Thank you for doing your absolute best to raise me in an environment of openness and acceptance. You both lifted me up with your words and your deeds. I know what love looks

The Book of Born Free - Volume One

because you showed me every day of my life. What up Roger?! We're brothers, let's connect and build more often. I love you! I also extend major love and electric appreciation to the rest of my beautiful family (Wharton and Lambert). What up ,Yen! (Yeeeennnie!!!) You have my love and you have my respect. I know we've been through more than a lot, but I'm sincerely grateful and appreciative for you and the life we've shared. Thank you for helping get this book done. Without your help, it wouldn't have been completed. That's a fact! You showed me clearly that I don't know what the hell a coma or a semi-colon is or how to use them. Lol! Love you forever! Big up to my brother from another mother, Mr. Wallace Ford. I treasure our friendship and brotherhood. Thanks for helping me with the graphic design of the cover. That was major! I'm still going to use that incredible picture you painted of me.

I have nothing but love for my Intelligent Muzik family (Wise Intelligent, Gino G, Masada, Courtney Danger (#dangerville), Rahzii Highpower, Shine, Tye Austin, Somer Lane, DJ Soyo, and Bigg Scott). No words can truly sum up with deep and abiding love and respect for you and all that you've brought into my life. Shout out to my brother Kalik Scientific for helping me stay on the path. I always love when we build and add on. I sincerely appreciate you and your light. My soul still needs a Cozmo Phyzix reading! Nothing but love goes out to Adrienne Lindsey (Ms. A), Nadria (DESS), Wynter, Mahal, and the one and only Nima Shiningstar-EL/Crystal Brown for shining your light on my path. And YO! Nima, I'm extremely proud of you and I love and respect you deeply. Narubi I love and appreciate you beyond words. You are definitely the Architect of Living Math. Plus laughing with you is one of the great joys in my life.

The Book of Born Free - Volume One

I also gotta acknowledge Miss Babz Rawls Ivy. Babz, I sincerely appreciate you and your belief in me and this project. And YO! I gotta say peace and thanks to Monique Danielle, Miss Tina Loris, and Aremjndi (check them out on Fiverr!). They came in deep in the last seconds of the 4th quarter and really helped me get this victory. Thanks Beloved, and let's continue to work and build! Last, but never least to all my friends and family (on and off social media), my peers, partners, lovers, teachers, supporters, fans, lovable stalkers, lyrical dance partners, my crazy and extremely tumblr crew, Tantric teachers, my spiritual advisors, story tellers, Elders, books, bookstores, libraries, poetry, all forms of music, Hip Hop Culture, my fantasies, sex, porn, masturbation, laughter, art, Ancestors, the sun, moon, and stars, my dreams, my visions, my loves, racism, sexism, white supremacy, governmental lies and cover-ups, cointelpro, intolerance, oppression, budget cuts, layoffs, domestic and foreign terrorism, GMO's, manufactured media, righteous police, wicked police, ignorance, and my faithful determined detractors. THANK YOU!

Without you, I wouldn't be who I am today. If you eliminate any one of these people, places, or things from my life (good or bad) I would be an entirely different expression and extension of The Most High. So, thank you sincerely for giving me all of you.

Now get ready for me to return the favor and then some!!!

Born Free #therealbornfree

The Book of Born Free - Volume One

MY OPENING STATEMENT

The Book of Born Free...The Wisdom of Living Right Now! is my truth. It represents my passions. It represents my dreams. It represents my political ideals. It represents my vision and experience of love. It represents my understanding of life. It represents my love of rap music and Hip-Hop Culture. It represents my complete and unwavering faith in the Creator of All the Worlds, Almighty YAH! This book, my book, represents the love that has lived vibrantly inside my heart-of-hearts for as long as I can remember. It represents my plan to help rebuild, re-educate, and re-embrace all those who have been broken down by this system of racist reduction. I want to help destroy the destroyers. I want to help guide you through this system of profit over people. I want to help wake folks up from this horrid unreality show version of love. Not to mention, we must get rid of all this corporate controlled musical mutilation and global spiritual degradation. We have a lot of work to do.

The idea of living right now is powerful to me, because it's always right now! We can't live in the right before or the right after; if we exist at all we exist right now! This is the space and time to activate whatever we're going to do with our lives. We have to take advantage of this fact and do something constructive to build a new and powerful architecture of freedom,
 fellowship, and faith. The urgency of this extremely pregnant moment is not lost on me. I've never been known as or thought of myself as an alarmist, but I am sounding the alarm! I am blowing the dog whistle!

The Book of Born Free - Volume One

I sincerely feel with every bone and blood cell in my body that we must come together as a human family and fight off the darkness right here and right now!

This book will give you a crystal-clear understanding of the 4-legs that hold up my prayer table, my bed, my kitchen table, and my home. For the last 30 plus years of my life I have loved and obsessed over "Politics and Culture", "Love/Sex and Relationships", "Hip-Hop Culture and Rap music", and "Philosophy and Spirituality". If you've been around me or have spoken with me for even a minute, you know all too well how I can get lost in these ideas and go on and on and on about them.

This book isn't about me explaining or justifying those ideas or qualifying why I am the way I am. It's about me expressing and exposing myself honestly in the light of this new day. The original idea was to give you 4 separate books over a 4 year period of time. I wanted to give each section of me room to breathe without being encumbered or crowded by my other parts. That idea faded away quickly because each section bleeds organically over into the next one, and I really don't have that kind of time to bullshit around and wait. The time is way too real! So, I broke them up into 2 volumes. The first volume deals with my unapologetic black perspective in relation to the current social and political climate and landscape. I also needed to have an open and extremely honest conversation about my view on love, relationships, intimacy, sex, loyalty, communication and compassion. The second volume will give you my Hip-Hop cultural perspective and my spiritual outlook on the world around us and inside of us.

The Book of Born Free - Volume One

The second volume will give you my Hip-Hop cultural perspective and my spiritual outlook on the world around us and inside of us. My political views and my attitudes towards love and sex are two sides of the same coin. For me, they feed off of each other. What happens in society has a direct connection to what happens in our personal relationships and what happens in our personal lives molds and shapes the kind human beings that will eventually occupy the power positions in the world. I wanted to start things off with the political shit because it will give you the proper context for everything else that I'm about to say and do.

Back in early 2008 the whole world was ablaze with nervous hope, jubilant paranoia, racist fever, and a form of blind faith that scared the shit out of me! Spiritually and mentally it was a really weird moment in time for me. It forced me to wonder if maybe, possibly, that America could finally live up to a small amount of her basic constitutional rhetoric.

Now don't get it twisted! I know that white supremacy isn't going anywhere. Racism, sexism, and intolerance aren't going anywhere. The insane and genocidal race

to amass the largest amount of death dealing weapons on the planet isn't going anywhere. The self-destructive force that propels us to disrupt the natural life sustaining ecosystems that support our natural existence, isn't going anywhere. I know this for a fact, but even with all my knowledge of self, I can admit

that I paused for a micro-second to ponder another reality.

The Book of Born Free - Volume One

I remember in 2007 when Wise Intelligent of the Legendary Poor Righteous Teachers was asked, if he thought that Obama would win, and if racism and

racial bias would finally be over as a result of his election. The blogger believed that we were about to enter into a true and genuine era of post-racial

America. Wise responded very directly by saying, "Obama

would not only win, but his election to the highest visible office in the land would give us (African-American's) a clear lesson and a brutally harsh reminder of what white supremacy and black dependency is all about". The blogger and the comments that followed Wise's statement chalked his beliefs up to pure cynicism. They wanted to believe

that the election of a black man to the presidency of the United of the States would be the beginning of black people finally gaining some true freedom, justice and equality in this society. They wanted to believe that Obama's election was more than just symbolic. In other words, they wanted to believe the beautiful lie.

Well, now that the Obama era is over, and the Trump reign is just beginning, many are echoing Wise's sentiments and praising his foresight. I'm not going to preempt myself by going into everything in my opening statement, but I will say this to be clear. I believe without a doubt that our position and condition in the black community has not improved enough to safely say that we as a people, as a collective group of human beings will be alright over the next few years, the next few months or even the next few minutes. From my unapologetic black perspective, we must

The Book of Born Free - Volume One

confront and kill white supremacy and the corresponding black dependency right now! I know that might seem extreme to some, but the reality is clear. Our children's future has not been secured. Our communities are still under attack from unrelenting police terrorism. We're still fighting and killing each other senselessly. We're still fighting off constant legislative assaults. We still haven't locked down enough land to supply our own demands. The physical and spiritual health of the black community is on life support. Now before you get depressed and separate yourself from what I'm saying, I will say on the positive side we have created a lot of individual institutions. We have a lot of local and independent networks, agencies, websites, schools, record labels, publishing houses, barber shops, beauty salons, fraternal and sorority clubs and various other businesses that are doing well, and I thank Almighty God for them. But we still have not linked together all those human resources to deal with our collective issues.

What did we really think Obama was going to do? Our dire situation will not be solved by one person at the plate swinging for the fences. I respect Obama and I love his family, but I'm saying that his election lulled us back to sleep! We weren't supposed to go into that voting booth (both times) and believe that by pressing a button (both times) that our journey towards true freedom, justice, and equality was over.

So, let me stop myself and allow all that to marinate and settle in while I give you a quick overview of the second section of this volume. I really love – love! I've always been a lover. Ask all the women that I've been blessed to have in my life and they'll tell you, that for

The Book of Born Free - Volume One

better or worse I am an extremely loving and deeply emotional person. I've always been very much in tune with my emotions and I have a high level of empathy that pours out into everything I say and do. I'm NOT SAYING I'M PERFECT AND THAT I HAVEN'T FUCKED UP A MILLION TIMES. I'm saying that at my core, my heart is true.

I was taught directly and indirectly that without a healthy and life affirming love, everything that we're attempting to do will be for naught. Look at the current status of love, sex, and relationships. Look at all the broken homes and broken people. Look at all our un-reality shows. Look at all our social media platforms. They don't show real love, they just bear witness to our hurt, pain, anger, disappointment, self-hate, greed, out of alignment lust, and a wickedly materialistic view of love. We've reduced our deepest expressions of love and the depth of our compassion to a series of Emjoi's and IG posts.

In isolation and looked at individually, it can seem like a series of small and unconnected things, but in the context of the rise of domestic violence, sexual harassment, college campus rape, and sexual assaults, I think that we need to stop and reassess what we're doing to ourselves and each other. I believe and feel without a shadow of a doubt that without a healthy, stable, and progressive view of love, sex, lust, family, and relationships, we are doomed as human beings. One of our primary and fundamental jobs on this planet is to co-create and build mutually beneficial social systems that have the real-time capacity to advance human life.

The Book of Born Free - Volume One

My definition of civilization has nothing to do with technology. A civilized person is a person that is civil in all their dealings. A civilized person is a person with a loving heart. A civilized person is a person who sees the whole and not just the parts. What does it matter if you have the newest phone, car, the most knowledge or the next generation technological marvel, if you're a certified asshole!!! Being an asshole renders everything else irrelevant. Especially if you're an asshole with global power and the ability to wield it as you see fit.

If we don't have a loving view of ourselves, our partners, and our environment, how can we co-create the kind of loving, compassionate, giving, and tolerant world that we say we want and desire. Without a healthy and loving relationship how can we hold our families together? How can we stop the violence? How can we stop our enemies at the gate?
We have to heal our relationships. We have to elevate our relationships. We have to supremely value our relationships. The love of self is vital and paramount in establishing a lasting and loving connection to another human being. Once you accept who and what you are, you are ready to enter into a truly compassionate union. A compassionate union is the foundation for any attempt to bring peace to this world. These beliefs have led me to have some incredible and dynamic experiences with the supreme loves of my life
From the time I was very young I was told and shown that a person cannot hope to rise up to the level of the eyesight of God without elevating the women around them. What follows is my love letter to all the beautiful black women who have loved me, held me, protected me, nurtured me, raised me, wrote poetry and rhymes with me, made love to me, fucked me, experimented

The Book of Born Free - Volume One

with me, danced with me, talked to me, walked with me, gone on trips with me, had phone sex with me, read books with me, debated me, congratulated me, cooked for me, encouraged me, pushed me, got mad at me, yelled at me, cursed at me, broke up with me, put me in my place, kicked me out, admonished me, rescued me, struggled with me, fought shoulder to shoulder with me, protested with me, laughed with me, prayed and meditated with me, and dreamed with me. I love you all deeply and honestly.

Thank you for taking time out of your life to plug into mine. After you finish reading and re-reading this work, find me online and let's build. Much Love Beloved!!!

Born Free #therealbornfree

The Book of Born Free - Volume One

INTRODUCTION

Enlightenment for many begins with that feeling you get when you're forced to view - differently - something you've been viewing, and in some cases living with, for decades without ever questioning your working interpretation of said phenomenon.

It's like when a child discovers that the fat, rosy-cheeked white guy with flying reindeer does not exist, and the gifts are really from their parents and loved ones. Initially the child is shocked, maybe even frightened by the revelation. However, the realization of the parents, family and friends love for the child is reinforced. This work is about love - love of community, love for a person, and love for humanity. The Book of Born Free...The Wisdom of Living Right Now! sets off an avalanche of critical thinking in the reader's mind that literally chases all of our social conditionings down the slope of reality-with the intention, to burry all of the dominate culture induced perceptions beneath a blizzard of cold, ice hard truth - unapologetically.

The Wisdom of Living Right Now! represents society's mirror, where in one glance the visage of ageless contradictions becomes old, tired, frail dust and ashes prepared to be blown away as the myth of Dorian Gray. Author, activist, artist manager, Hip Hop ambassador, and father - Born Free masterfully challenges the reader to think beyond the clichés, catch phrases, outright lies, governmental misdirection's, self-destructive stereotypes, pure bullshit, and indoctrinating mainstream themes, which have calcified within our consciousness, without ever attacking or condemning the beliefs of any.

The Book of Born Free - Volume One

This book of insightful quotes might have been written by a passionately proud and extremely African-Centered African-American man but its appeal is completely universal and intensely rooted in the global human experience.

Born Free is the pulmonary specialist carefully performing a psychological angioplasty removing the plaque of "popular opinion", "scholastic miseducation", "musical inebriation" "repressed emotions", "inhibited sexual urges", and "political correctness" from the arteries of our spiritual bodies so that truth may once more flow freely, uncensored, unfettered, and unimpeded. Each quote is timeless and will give you more clarity each time that you read them.

Some of Born's thoughts will make you laugh, some will make you cry, some will make you angry, some will make you feel safe and secure, some will make you fight back, some will make you forgive and heal, some will make you feel proud, some will make you feel uneasy, some will make you feel loved, and some will make your spirit soar. But all of them will make you think deeply about the world around you and inside of you in a new and exciting way. Like a sober uncle with a drunken uncle's audacity, like a tried and tested military veteran-the lessons are clear, unnerving, and direct. Born doesn't hold back or bite his tongue and boldly stands by each and every one of his statements and opinions. As I was reading through this lyrical labyrinth of high self-esteem and enhanced racial pride, the main theme of active activism is screaming at the top of itself lungs from every page.

The Book of Born Free - Volume One

Born doesn't want us to just read his words and memorize his quotes. He wants us to stand up and make a positive difference in our lives and the lives of OUR children, community, and THIS world. For Born Free this is the true and only purpose of Living Right Now!

The Book of Born Free...The Wisdom of Living Right Now! WILL help us see things clearly for what they are and not what they present themselves to be. We need these jewels now more than ever.

Wise Intelligent
(Poor Righteous Teachers)

The Book of Born Free - Volume One

what do we really want?
what do we really believe?
what are we really trying to do?
what we are really trying to achieve?
the more I ponder
the more these questions assault my sleep
but I stay deep within the breech
because faith is an unending leap

Born Free #therealbornfree

The Book of Born Free - Volume One

***My
Unapologetic
Black Perspective
and the
Political Ramifications
of
Living Right Now!***

The Book of Born Free - Volume One

NOT A DISCLAIMER

*this is my UNAPOLOGETIC
black perspective
each thought manifested
has been blessed and tested
agree or disagree
it's all me
I'm here to do more
than just spill the tea
I guarantee
each of these decrees
will feel like the degrees
we pulled from the deep dead seas
these are new major keys
to open old slave locks
to cure the smallpox
they placed in the ballot box
I'm a paradox
unorthodox
I'm Vandana Shiva
here to seed the crops
I can't be stopped
fuck a roadblock
I write like Amos Wilson
brainstorming with the Lox
some thoughts are vibrant
like the feathers on peacocks
some thoughts are dark
like the barrels inside twin Glocks
but like it or not
this is my truth
this is my testimony
this is my proof
this is my life
this is my analysis
this is my honest attempt
to break the paralysis
expose the savageness
political flatulence*

The Book of Born Free - Volume One

show you that white supremacy
is no fuckin accident
land and resources were taken
all lives were forsaken
white supremacy and white racism
comes from the grafted heart of Satan
challenge me
challenge my stance
challenge my call
for humanity to advance
cuz I go deeper than skin color
I'm talkin conscious behavior
hateful natures
my truth cuts like rusty razors
I'm not doin any favors
cuz you can't be my neighbor
or the face of the savior
if you're a mother fuckin slave traitor
no more waivers
no more false layers
no more political
hypocritical peace makers
so, turn the page
burn some sage
and let's come together
to usher in a new age

Born Free #therealbornfree

The Book of Born Free - Volume One

(Jewel #1)
once we open the door and soar
the light will envelop us all
enthralled
our souls will slowly start to thaw
everyone screams for revelation
but who really wants to be revealed
no eye will remain dry
once this onion gets peeled

(Jewel #2)
your revolution can't be sponsored
by your oppressor
you can't talk to God
through your molester
you can't depend on your abuser
for your wealth and good health
and you can't use your slave master's definitions
to define yourself

(Jewel #3)
while we occupy the streets
they occupy our minds and limbs
the eviction without
starts with the exorcism within
protesting is necessary
but we need to move with a greater strategy
or stay stuck on this treadmill
reacting to tragedy after tragedy

The Book of Born Free - Volume One

(Jewel #4)
over 750 people murdered in Chicago
by the end of December
family members dismembered
in the bloodiest year to remember
the FEDS were called in
to lock the whole town down
this is the only solution
when the victims are black and brown

(Jewel #5)
the die is cast
the bubbles have burst
have no fear
our ancestors survived worse
you're not cursed
build, and organize
galvanize your family
and RISE!

The Book of Born Free - Volume One

(Jewel #6)
the Arab Spring
is evolving into the winter of our discontent
I'm bent because two working parents
still can't pay the fucking rent
change isn't a presidential slogan
or a commercial phrase
change is revolution
and we've just entered the first stage

(Jewel #7)
if we don't turn up
we're going to keep getting turned out
scream, shout
we can't afford another financial drought
mobilize, prioritize
and stop the infighting
cuz if these racists keep recycling
the next few lifetimes will be frightening

(Jewel #8)
let's cultivate and harvest
this pregnant proactive protest
use our access
to get some actual redress
let's force them to deal
with the real root cause
our collective unity
can change unjust policies and laws

The Book of Born Free - Volume One

(Jewel #9)
some say I'm desperate
some say I'm ineffective
I SAY
I'm giving you my unapologetic black perspective
some enthusiastically agree
others vigorously object
I don't fret
I have no guilt or regret

(Jewel #10)
if Katrina didn't convince you
you're truly beyond help
Katrina was the clearest example
of why we must provide for ourselves
do I need to dwell on Sandy
Harvey, Irma, Maria, and Jose?
your children will only be okay
if you prepare for the worse today

The Book of Born Free - Volume One

(Jewel #11)
back on November 4th, 2008
I felt the earth shake
Barack Hussein Obama
became the 44th President of the United States
we combined as we witnessed
this historic moment in time
but sadly having a black president
rendered us deaf, dumb, and blind

(Jewel #12)
if we can't examine Obama's policies
like we aggressively did with Bush
what's the point
of this new democratic push
the presidency isn't personal
this needs to be clear to us
there's too much on the line
to co-sign a blank check or blind trust

(Jewel #13)
as soon as it was clear
that Obama would succeed
state after state
put in petitions to secede
do you see what I see?
these lessons are too clear
we better fortify our position
before they force us out of here

(Jewel #14)
I didn't expect Obama
to score all the points
I didn't expect Obama
to grab all the black babies and anoint
but I didn't expect him to be
so hawkish on war, trade, and drones
or make the white house
Wall Street's home away from home

(Jewel #15)
I respect Obama
as an intelligent black man
it must be stressful as hell
to command The Blue Klux Klan
Michelle's an intelligent black woman
of the highest distinction
it must be stressful as hell
to work with those who want our extinction

The Book of Born Free - Volume One

(Jewel #16)
on November 7th, 2012
the universe began to violently vibrate
Barack Hussein Obama
retained the presidency of the United States
the white community found unity
and revealed their true mind
but sadly
we're still deaf, dumb, and blind

(Jewel #17)
Obama's cultural cadence
has the silence of surveillance
his Wall Street acquaintance
has a putrid fragrance
the audacity
of his undeniable eloquence
became embarrassingly impotent
in white supremacy's direct presence

(Jewel #18)
I can't afford bedroom slippers
I've retired my marching shoes
don't talk that complaining shit
like we haven't paid the ultimate dues
Israel didn't march one step
to get 3 BILLION in government aid
the community put you first
now we're the last ones getting paid

The Book of Born Free - Volume One

(Jewel #19)
Obama said if Israel is weakened
it would be a failure of his presidency
I wonder if he felt the same
about a weakened black community
does our vulnerability
endear the same vocal affinity
does our weakened stability
get the same presidential urgency

(Jewel #20)
I AM Barack Obama
whether I agree with his every step or not
I won't passively sit back
and watch another black leader get shot
he's an absolute inspiration
to the next generation of our children
and I'll help burn this country down
if you try to hurt or kill him

The Book of Born Free - Volume One

(Jewel #21)
Democrat or Republican
the power structure remains the same
how many more seasons
will we play this Orwellian game
voting is a privilege
but it's mostly leverage
but most of us use it
like it's an alcoholic beverage

(Jewel #22)
voting is one way
but it's not the only way
we need to apply all kinds of pressure
a strategic squeeze play
what are we trying to gain
where are we trying to aim
time and land lost
isn't so easily reclaimed

(Jewel #23)
our dependence makes us more than weak
it makes us a villain
ready and willin'
to betray our children
it makes us sit when we should stand
beg when we should take
our dependence makes God's people
move and act like snakes

The Book of Born Free - Volume One

(Jewel #24)
first it's all about the votes
then it's all about the delegates
and after the delegates
it's all about the college electorate
it's all rhetoric
the rebranding of a confederate
look at the evidence
it's all venomous

(Jewel #25)
if you choose to vote
then vote
but don't get mad at my quotes
if it's not the final antidote
I'm not going to stop you
if that's what you want to promote
but don't be sad and sulk
if they sign in crayon on your promissory note

The Book of Born Free - Volume One

(Jewel #26)
street credibility
isn't more important than personal integrity
don't let adversity or jealousy
take you away from your destiny
if your friends can't see
beyond felonies or complacency
just keep moving forward
towards the farthest galaxy

(Jewel #27)
I can't hug the block with you
I'm too busy hugging my seed
providing for her needs
making up for past deeds
that culture isn't for me
it's a path I wish you didn't take
my heart breaks
cuz that's a decision that you must make

(Jewel #28)
your plan is only as good
as your execution
just like your facts are not facts
if they can't be shown and proven
get movin'
get deep down in the dirt
cuz if you plan to eat
you better plan to work

The Book of Born Free - Volume One

(Jewel #29)
stagnant knowledge
is wickedness at work
it might make you feel intelligent
but it will get you critically hurt
if you don't put your thoughts in motion
they will decay your mind
and reading all those books
will amount to a tremendous waste of time

(Jewel #30)
if you refuse to get or create a job
don't blame PTSS or PTSD
if you refuse to pay child support
don't charge it to 400 years of slavery
oppression, racism, and apple pie
will always be the American way
but those are not the reasons
why you're disrespected and alone today

The Book of Born Free - Volume One

(Jewel #31)
you don't owe the street anything
you're more than your block
who's going to hold your family down
if you get knocked and locked
who's going to provide for your children
while you're doing 25 to life
and who's going to be the one
satisfying the needs of your wife

(Jewel #32)
I don't care about your tats
or you pulling your pants up
my main concern
is that you get those damn grades up
getting a quality education
is more than just good advice
cuz when your mind is sharp
you can cut out a nice slice of life

(Jewel #33)
most poor children
have no time for lectures and speeches
money by any means necessary
is the only message that reaches
they worship a platinum Jesus
with European features
cuz their parents, preachers and teachers
treated them like creatures

The Book of Born Free - Volume One

(Jewel #34)
I understand the game
but I don't believe it's worth it
how many must die
before you question the purpose
all these material things
barely scratch the earth's surface
and become spiritual burdens
at your friend's funeral service

(Jewel #35)
I'm not anti-anybody
all are welcome to break bread
but I won't let you
run a game on my head
the unbalanced power relations displayed
has everyone in doubt and afraid
and until it's dead in a grave decayed
I'll continue to expose the masquerade

The Book of Born Free - Volume One

(Jewel #36)
they said Michael Brown stole cigars
so, he deserved to get smoked
the officer wasn't at fault
because he was provoked
this sick, twisted blame-the-victim logic
is a devilish slope
Satan, remove the cloak
9-1-1 is still a mother fuckin' joke

(Jewel #37)
do black kids commit crimes
and other serious offenses? Absolutely!
do white kids commit crimes
and other serious offenses? Absolutely!
but in the eyes of the law
black and white kids aren't treated the same
white kids get arraigned
black kids get a bullet in the brain

(Jewel #38)
we all knew (insert cop's name)
wasn't going to be indicted
riot ignited
every day we're horrifically reminded
the ball is in our court
they've made their decisions
either we activate our activism
or prepare for more death and prison

The Book of Born Free - Volume One

(Jewel #39)
thousands are in the street
but passion must give way to a direction
a lasting connection
will make this a true insurrection
some condemn
but without this visible aggression and dissension
another life would be lost
and no one would be paying attention

(Jewel #40)
remember Tarika Wilson
remember Aiyana Jones
don't let their memories
fade away with their bones
honor them
don't put them in the forgotten archives
never forget the day
these beasts viciously took away their lives

The Book of Born Free - Volume One

(Jewel #41)
remember Eleanor Bumpurs
remember Tyisha Miller
don't let their true light be extinguished
by these unlawful killers
remember their story
not a statistical category
they were flesh and blood
not an abstract allegory

(Jewel #42)
if I'm guilty, I'll get shot
if I'm innocent, I'll get shot
if I have a gun, I'll get shot
if I don't have a gun, I'll get shot
if I run, I'll get shot
if I don't run, I'll get shot
if I have my hands down, I'll get shot
if I have my hands up, I'll get shot

(Jewel #43)
Charles Kinsey was lying flat on his back
arms outstretched
they still claimed he was a threat
he still got wet
how fuckin innocent can you get
he didn't resist
this is bullshit
they want us dead and that's it

The Book of Born Free - Volume One

(Jewel #44)
if they allude
that I look like a "bad dude"
does that justify my murder
by the boys and girls in blue
how did they prove
that Terence Crutcher was a "bad dude"
but who cares when you're pursued as food
by the boys and girls in blue

(Jewel #45)
it's time to close the door
on our petty tribal wars
it was tribal wars
that helped put us on all fours
fighting each other over local customs
and beliefs makes us weak
and makes it easy for crooked police
to shoot us dead in the street

The Book of Born Free - Volume One

(Jewel #46)
that piece of shit George Zimmerman
was acquitted of all charges
how long will America be lost
in this forest of racial darkness
Trayvon was profiled
judged, and executed all at the same time
and walking home while black
was his only American crime

(Jewel #47)
they say, we kill each other
so, don't complain when others do the same
we're to blame
and we should hang our heads in shame
but whites kill whites
Asians kill Asians, and Jews kill Jews
but has that EVER given me and you
the right and hall pass to kill them too

(Jewel #48)
what happened in Dallas and Baton Rouge
was tragic, no excuses
but this is the hate
that hate produces
when the Blue Klux Klan
goes on patrol and puts holes in your soul
revenge comes in
and the whole population explodes

The Book of Born Free - Volume One

(Jewel #49)
how many black cops profile
white kids as skinheads and neo Nazis
and assume confederate flags & Swastikas
is a threat to civilized society
how many black cops execute
because of uncertainty and fear
and how many black cops
would be cleared by a jury of their peers

(Jewel #50)
not guilty! not guilty!
the echoes won't let go
young black kids dying senselessly
in and out the ghetto
by white hands, black hands
individuals, and governments
the devil is loving it
cuz murder and hate strengthens his covenant

The Book of Born Free - Volume One

(Jewel #51)
you can't rob and kill your own
and then complain about killer cops
because like it or not
you BOTH must be stopped
internal violence is the oxygen
that keeps police terrorism alive
you BOTH must die
if we are to survive

(Jewel #52)
I don't fuck with black on black murderers
savage hamburglars
I teach young black learners
and older Ivan Van Sertima's
while you mumble and murmur
I'm moving forward with the merger
a reader and a worker
going beyond the online fervor

(Jewel #53)
it might look like this rich nigga lifestyle
is profitable and seductive
but it's destructive
that shit is so unproductive
this ignorant transformation
makes it impossible for us to win
cuz I've never met a real nigga
who was a good father, husband, or friend

The Book of Born Free - Volume One

(Jewel #54)
I know when you point your gun
you think you have the upper hand
and when you see the fear in his eyes
you feel like the bigger man
but the sad news is that you and your crew
are being used
to hold our community back
and keep us terrorized and abused

(Jewel #55)
it's hard to stand like a man
when you're financially on your knees
you better learn how to separate
your wants from your needs
if you want to succeed
activate your plans
get the fuck off your ass
and start using your divine mind and earthly hands

The Book of Born Free - Volume One

(Jewel #56)
niggas were manufactured
and created to be at odds
they were cultivated and raised
to destroy the movements of God
niggas were used to kill Malcolm
they were used to kill Huey
niggas were manufactured
to kill Tupac and Biggie

(Jewel #57)
look at the murder rates in Philly
being a nigga doesn't work!
look at the murder rates in Chicago
being a nigga doesn't work!
look at the murder rates in New Orleans
being a nigga doesn't work!
look at all the inner-city murder rates
being a nigga doesn't work!

(Jewel #58)
some become savages unknown
self-hate deep in their bones
invading their neighbor's homes
young death in school zones
and the reason we stand so unrepentant
in the face of a long sentence
the knowledge of OUR God
has been stripped from our remembrance

The Book of Born Free - Volume One

(Jewel #59)
I'm not here to blindly judge niggas
or blindly judge thugs
I'm here as your brother
trying to show you true God love
but I don't see you as niggas
or angry black bitches
I think we got lost and twisted
trying to go from rags to riches

(Jewel #60)
I hate the fact that
we believe we're niggas
I hate white supremacy
for turning us into niggas
I hate black leaders who took money
to become the white man's bottom nigga
I hate the fact that we didn't embrace
and love these beautiful and broken lost niggas

The Book of Born Free - Volume One

(Jewel #61)
where are all the panels
and new IG twitter trends
about the epidemic of old white men
molesting innocent young white children
every day a political priest
takes a child across that devilish line
when will they take responsibility
for this epidemic white on white crime

(Jewel #62)
doctors with script pads are just as bad
as dealers with a crack in bags
so many predator crabs
work in government-funded labs
you can't hide your foul stench
with chlorine and Lysol
prescription drugs kill more adults and teens
than PCP and 8-Ball

(Jewel #63)
when a white person does a crime
they're an individual
when a black person does a crime
the whole culture is criminal
white people do heroin they bring in counselors
it's a social sickness
black people do crack they bring in SWAT
and shoot with the quickness

The Book of Born Free - Volume One

(Jewel #64)
if you're white you can use Affluenza
as an excuse for your crimes
but if you're black you can't use your poverty
to reduce your time
it's all hypocritical
parasitical, political
so when Casey Anthony was set free
I just said fuckin typical

(Jewel #65)
a healthy skepticism
and cynicism
is godly wisdom when dealing with
a debased system
when they call me paranoid
I don't get annoyed
I don't fall for the ploy
I'm trying to stop us from being destroyed

The Book of Born Free - Volume One

(Jewel #66)
was Roger Ailes race relevant
to the sexual harassment investigation
is Josh Duggar race relevant
to his molestation investigation
is Bill O'Reilly's race relevant
to his sick serial sexual misconduct
when the criminal is white
race and culture are never brought up

(Jewel #67)
from Jimmy Savile
to Jared Fogle
the sexual assault of children
is grotesque and global
these celebrity predators
are social Chernobyl's
I support the complete disposal
of all these monster moguls

(Jewel #68)
Dr. Seuss was a racist
you say how can that BE
cuz HE didn't like humans
who looked like ME
Dr. Seuss wasn't IMMUNE
his racism blossomed and BLOOMED
he made racist CARTOONS
to make US look like BUFFOONS

The Book of Born Free - Volume One

(Jewel #69)
white people still look at me
as I walk up and down the aisle
clutch their purses
and flash me a nervous smile
I'm still their first bet for crime
violence and calamity
and they're still shocked when a white man
goes home and kills his entire suburban family

(Jewel #70)
if the white community could get over
their racism a little bit faster
they might be able to see the signs
of the next bloody movie massacre
but since they can't stop seeing blacks
as the main criminals on earth
the crime within their own communities
eludes their so-called search

The Book of Born Free - Volume One

(Jewel #71)
in 2018 many whites say
we're hateful and ungrateful
and kneeling during the anthem
is utterly disgraceful
but I don't give a fuck
about their shameful appraisal
I'm the child of America's slave legacy
of bullshit and betrayal

(Jewel #72)
in 2018 many whites wonder
why blacks aren't satisfied
a black president should have
healed the racial divide
but the issues of race aren't based
on having a single good job
unequal power relations
brings forth the wrath of God

(Jewel #73)
in 2018 many whites refuse
to factor in the historical context
they call it suspect
and say it has no relevance
they act like a 400-year head start
is fair and even
and that's why the revolution
will always be in season

The Book of Born Free - Volume One

(Jewel #74)
in 2018 many whites still believe
in manifest destiny
and slavery while horrible
was an absolute necessity
they still see America
as a shining city upon a hill
they can't deal
with the millions upon millions they've killed

(Jewel #75)
in 2018 many whites can't see
that they're the recipient of a cursed gift
and all those dead spirits
refuse to be dismissed
white control of land, water and air
didn't emerge from thin air
white freedom and happiness
was paid for by black-death and despair

The Book of Born Free - Volume One

(Jewel #76)
in 2018 many whites point to black celebrities
as the changing times
as if George Clooney's money
keeps all whites off the breadline
when they see Jay Z and B
they ignore the economic gravity
of planned poverty
and systematic legislative depravity

(Jewel #77)
in 2018 many whites blame the government
for a lack of opportunities
Wall Street conspiracy theories
are driving them towards a nationwide mutiny
they want Donald Chump
to get militant and fix it
and blame all white problems on
Muslims and undocumented immigrants

(Jewel #78)
in 2018 many whites feel forgotten
and left behind
maligned and purposefully pushed out
of America's sunshine
they say it's all Obama's fault
it's all NAFTA's fault
but nobody ever tells them to halt
cuz all their failures are their fault

The Book of Born Free - Volume One

(Jewel #79)
in 2018 many whites are calling for
open revolution as the solution
jobs leaving the country
forced them to that conclusion
domestic violence is on the rise
Opioids are their drug of choice
but nobody tells them to stop complaining
when they use their whining voice

(Jewel #80)
in 2018 many whites refuse
to walk or talk softly
so in 2016
they voted in King Joffrey
off with their undocumented heads
off with the head of Roe v. Wade
ignorance and anti-feminism
are at the front of America's parade unafraid

The Book of Born Free - Volume One

(Jewel #81)
it's time to kill the leviathan
of domestic violence
no more compliance
no more silence
no more protections for those
who commit wicked transgressions
no matter the practice or profession
you're going to face a hard-fuckin lesson

(Jewel #82)
the NFL isn't the only one
with a Roethlisberger within its ranks
organized sports reaction to sexual assault
is connected to the bank
if public backlash takes away cash
they'll deal swift and fast
but if the headlines fade and pass
they'll file your pain away in the trash

(Jewel #83)
don't try to debate or relate
a new definition of rape
it doesn't matter if she was knocked out
or wide awake
rape is rape
a barbaric and brutal crime
rape is the murder
of the mind, body, soul, and time

The Book of Born Free - Volume One

(Jewel #84)
how come the worse kinds of men
have the greatest power to deceive
how come the most brutalized women
are never believed
I'm not trying to be rhetorical
I'm not trying to be poetic
the rape culture in America
is disgusting and pathetic

(Jewel #85)
on or offline nudity
isn't consent
short dresses and no panties
don't imply intent
drugging away her memory
doesn't make it any less of a heinous act
and rape charges
shouldn't have a short-term contract

The Book of Born Free - Volume One

(Jewel #86)
if they're beating you
leave them
if they apologize again and again
don't believe them
I do believe people can change
I do believe in redemption
but walking away from an abuser
is the best prevention

(Jewel #87)
if love were easy
it wouldn't be of use
but if your love draws blood
then its abuse
if the one you love shows their love
with a threat, a hit, and a shove
beloved, what you call love
really isn't love

(Jewel #88)
don't try to rationalize
the slap
don't try to rationalize
the attack
don't try to understand his hard day
and family background
just pack your bags
and get the fuck out of town

The Book of Born Free - Volume One

(Jewel #89)
if he hits you
let someone know
if she hits you
let someone know
abusers use silence and isolation
to gain strength and momentum
they use everything you don't mention
as a wicked new weapon

(Jewel #90)
your new and wonderful life
started today
it happened the moment you decided
to walk away
it started the moment that you decided
to take your power back
it started the moment you walked out
and never looked back

The Book of Born Free - Volume One

(Jewel #91)
if black women are being abused
I'm being abused
if I let her hand go
we all lose
even though a black man's face
has been the logo of the movement
without black women
there's no hope for improvement

(Jewel #92)
don't let black women
be muted or marginalized
chastised or despised
lift them up to the sky
open your heart to them
beloved love them
when they ascend
we all ascend

(Jewel #93)
Queen, I'm not your enemy
or your downfall
please don't believe
that I will ignore your call
I've made mistakes
I haven't always been awake
but in the end, we'll celebrate
the bonfire of grafted snakes

The Book of Born Free - Volume One

(Jewel #94)
it's not just about black men
black women aren't spared
the war against her
has also been declared
the number of women killed by police
is downright scary
don't tarry
they want us all dead and buried

(Jewel #95)
without a strong black family
we're doomed before we commence
that's the reason white supremacy
put us on opposite sides of the fence
that's why they love when we fight
and tear each other down
white supremacy knows that
only strong families get to wear the crown

The Book of Born Free - Volume One

(Jewel #96)
if we want to preserve our families
we must intimately coalesce
be blessed
mine out destiny's best
every man, woman, and child
has a serious job to do
together is the only way
we'll get through

(Jewel #97)
you can't raise a strong black family
without a cultural component
an African-Centered enrollment
enables you to seize the moment
your history is your present
your present is your future
study why your people
were the world's first rulers

(Jewel #98)
create your own educational system
based on the needs of your people
education doesn't have to be the same
to be equal
you need Sanchez before Shakespeare
Dunbar before Whitman
Brooks before Milton
and Marley before Dylan

The Book of Born Free - Volume One

(Jewel #99)
create your own financial system
based on the needs of your people
the American banking system
has been historically deceitful
invest in yourself
invest in your own platforms
this is how nations survive
economic storms

(Jewel #100)
wake up! wake up!
and STAY WOKE!
it's time to move beyond
the joke of the popular vote
depending on the outcomes
of debates and elections
puts our children's future
in jeopardy and in question

The Book of Born Free - Volume One

(Jewel #101)
I'm an original black man
I'm a strong black man
I'm a loving black man
I'm an intelligent black man

(Jewel #102)
I'm a I-love-my-black-woman-black man
I'm a I-love-my-black-family-black man
I'm a saving black man
I'm a planning black man

(Jewel #103)
I'm an activist black man
I'm a builder black man
I'm a sustainer black man
I'm a protector black man

(Jewel #104)
I'm an old school black man
I'm an up-to-date black man
I'm a tomorrow black man
I'm a next century black man

(Jewel #105)
I'm a fatherly black man
I'm an understanding black man
I'm a compassionate black man
I'm a truthful black man

The Book of Born Free - Volume One

(Jewel #106)
I'm a flawed black man
I'm a conflicted black man
I'm a perplexed black man
I'm a hurting black man

(Jewel #107)
I'm an aggressive black man
I'm a broken-hearted black man
I'm an impulsive black man
I'm a defensive black man

(Jewel #108)
I'm a scornful black man
I'm a sarcastic black man
I'm a weird black man
I'm an off-center black man

(Jewel #109)
I'm an opinionated black man
I'm a conceited black man
I'm an impatient black man
I'm a complicated black man

(Jewel #110)
I'm a I-did-my-fair-share-of-dirt black man
I'm an imperfect black man
I'm a corrupted black man
I'm a fallible black man

The Book of Born Free - Volume One

(Jewel #111)
I'm a reading black man
I'm a visionary black man
I'm a sensual black man
I'm an erotic black man

(Jewel #112)
I'm an African black man
I'm a Hebrew Israelite black man
I'm a I-love-my-African-people black man
I'm a black nationalist black man

(Jewel #113)
I'm a frontline black man
I'm a warrior black man
I'm a gun-in-hand black man
I'm a peaceful black man

(Jewel #114)
I'm a Hip-Hop black man
I'm a soulful black man
I'm a jazzy black man
I'm a blues black man

(Jewel #115)
I'm a prayerful black man
I'm a Christ conscious black man
I'm a deeply spiritual Torah reading black man
I'm a God fearing and God loving black man

The Book of Born Free - Volume One

(Jewel #116)
kill the irrelevant noise
either we build or destroy
Nigeria #BringBackOurGirls
Vatican #StopMolestingOurBoys
it's a war against the poor
a war against the youth
and our paralyzing fear
stops us from confronting these horrible truths

(Jewel #117)
terror in Charleston, Baltimore
Ferguson, Orlando, Paris
these soulless bastards
want to destroy all that we cherish
the sacred womb of a church
the abundant joy of a concert hall
the goal of these devils
is to destroy us all

(Jewel #118)
ISIS claimed responsibility
but don't blame ALL of Islam
we never blamed ALL of Christianity
for Eric Rudolph's bombs
ISIS is evil
and that's not contestable
but labeling all Muslims as terrorists
is detestable

The Book of Born Free - Volume One

(Jewel #119)
ISIS reminds me every day
just how insane insanity can be
this repulsive brutality
would make Satan blush and flee
America reminds me every day
just how hypocritical hypocrisy can be
this demonistic democracy
is gonna make God kill us to set us free

(Jewel #120)
I still have faith
even though my thoughts seem to contradict
evil's eclipse
is something that only God can fix
I'm not saying I'm not angry
or I wouldn't hit back
I'm saying evil hasn't consumed my soul
in these horrid attacks

The Book of Born Free - Volume One

(Jewel #121)
whites want to say nigga
but for centuries they couldn't say brother
they preyed on our prayers
and captured us like savage hunters
why do you want to say it
we say it because of Mentacide
why do you want to water the hatred
that your ancestors planted deep inside

(Jewel #122)
the whole country doesn't have to be racist
for it to be a racist society
racism is when one group
controls the military and the economy
the means of production
and the ability to turn the key and knob
racism is praying to someone else's
concept of God

(Jewel #123)
don't call my passionate fight for justice
a cold and petty revenge
it's an intoxicating love for self
on a serious binge
the fire in my belly
is tempered by Coltrane's Love Supreme
this isn't just about protecting our bodies
we're fighting for our dreams

The Book of Born Free - Volume One

(Jewel #124)
you can't have a standardized test
without standardized funds
America benefits from us
being ignorant and dumb
they said No Child Left behind
then they financially turn their backs
flooded the inner city with illegal guns
outdated books, wack rap, and crack

(Jewel #125)
I'm crying because I'm in love
I'm crying because I'm invested
I don't regret crying
because it's a part of being tested
I'm laughing because I'm happy
I'm laughing because life's absurd
I'll never stop laughing
because despair can't have the final word

The Book of Born Free - Volume One

(Jewel #126)
this black leadership is too scared
too ensnared
unprepared
too comfortable bent over that chair
they wouldn't dare
move a timid toe out of line
how can a cuckold concubine
protect you, me, and mine

(Jewel #127)
I want us to stop asking
to take down the confederate flag
I want us to get together
and start ripping down that confederate flag
and once we get that out of the way
let's dig deeper in the bag
and deal with what we've experienced
under the American flag

(Jewel #128)
they slam our daughters
out of their desk
remind us every day
that we're still oppressed
they use the threat of death
when we disturb the peace
but after white bikers kill at twin peaks
they got to FaceTime, IG, and tweet

The Book of Born Free - Volume One

(Jewel #129)
you can't drink the water in Flint
you can't drink the water in Trenton
you can't drink the water
in all the other cities they didn't mention
our ancestors warned us
but we chose the oppressor's paper chase
now we're begging for help from the same people
who fucked us over in the first place

(Jewel #130)
where is OUR
NAFTA and GATT
where is OUR
Marshall Plan at
where is OUR
TPP and CETA
it's getting too late in the day
to still be begging this way

The Book of Born Free - Volume One

(Jewel #131)
they say it's not about black or white
it's all about the green
but you get more green
when you move like a team
every racial group uses their cultural unity
as leverage and tool
to build a solid infrastructure
to extend their rule

(Jewel #132)
they say today's financial crisis
is worse than the Great Depression
why does it take a 30-year recession
for us to accept some old lessons
the black community is the most vulnerable
cuz we're the most dependent
when the civil liberties get revoked
ours will be quickly suspended

(Jewel #133)
we vote
and then we beg
we beg
and then we complain
we complain
and then turn to apathy
and after apathy
we implode in our community

The Book of Born Free - Volume One

(Jewel #134)
just because I advocate for us
to control our own nation
doesn't mean I want to sit aimless
under the tree of isolation
I believe in diverse communication
intimate global human relations
but it's self-castration
to forsake our own foundation

(Jewel #135)
racism isn't a good enough reason
for you to fold your hand
racism didn't stop our ancestors
from making a glorious stand
racism can't stop you from being
Christ like and humanly powerful
racism is just another obstacle
not a mission impossible

The Book of Born Free - Volume One

(Jewel #136)
the myth of American exceptionalism
is quickly unraveling
we can't ignore the broken-hearted bodies
on the road we're traveling
they are the believers, the voters
and the everyday achievers
who were all blindsided
by gilded golden-tongued deceivers

(Jewel #137)
America's always tortured
drawn, and quartered
pillaged the village
murdered and slaughtered
lynched and bombed
and had centuries of false recording
so why second guess
if they're capable of rendition and water boarding

(Jewel #138)
America can't be indicted
for all the negativity in the world
America isn't at fault
for every hungry little boy and girl
but America's hands are so bloody
when it comes to its procedures
you must always question
the policies of its leaders

The Book of Born Free - Volume One

(Jewel #139)
living under drones
living as drones
we've chosen
to make the known unknown
these mechanical abominations
are unmanned and unsouled
the story is no longer told
about for whom the bell tolls

(Jewel #140)
6 billion isn't a campaign donation
it's a political investment
if you've forgotten how governments
work re-read the New Testament
and now that Dark Money
is coming into the light
you'll see there's no real difference
between the left and the right

The Book of Born Free - Volume One

(Jewel #141)
we argue over colors
we argue over the streets
we argue over styles
we argue over beats
we argue over war
we argue over peace
all this arguing
is the clearest mark of the beast

(Jewel #142)
all our youth aren't innocent
or above correction
but they certainly weren't born evil
or beyond God's redemption
and if we're not giving them the means
what do we really mean
we love them, or we don't
there's no in between

(Jewel #143)
another group of potential Messiah's
was murdered in Philly last night
the devil's acolyte's delight
in fresh death right after twilight
we need more than positive role models
and after school programs
we need to know how to rebuild
a spiritually broken woman and man

The Book of Born Free - Volume One

(Jewel #144)
the black degradation must stop
the backbiting must stop
the trap glorification must stop
the domestic abuse must stop
the ignorance must stop
the laziness must stop
the drug abuse must stop
the nigga-bitch shit must stop

(Jewel #145)
we're not going to get
what we're begging for
we're not going to get
what we're crawling for
we're not going to get
what we're selling out for
we're not going to get what
we're killing ourselves for

The Book of Born Free - Volume One

(Jewel #146)
when your daddy is in the streets
and your mother smokes crack
your brother gang bangs
and your sister loves the trap
when your friends sell drugs
and you're the dead weight of the state
how do you change your fate
when you're born behind the eight

(Jewel #147)
he heard his mom say
"nigga, where the fuck you been?!"
she heard her dad say
"bitch don't start that bullshit again!"
20 years later his son heard him say
"bitch what you gonna do?"
her daughter heard her mom load the gun
and say, "nigga fuck you!"

(Jewel #148)
no one wants to live like a nigga
not even the most niggerish
they know it's bullshit
and completely ridiculous
but when you're raised in the mix
of guns, drugs, and tricks politics
you slide in the clip after reading
the world is yours off the side of a blimp

The Book of Born Free - Volume One

(Jewel #149)
I believe in personal responsibility
but tell the whole story
don't ignore me, whore me
or forget what happened before me
when I was just a baby
the whole world made my decisions
instead of building me a new school
they invested in better prisons

(Jewel #150)
I'm not playing victim
because I speak about being victimized
suppressing my feelings
can lead to mass suicide and homicide
when I speak about my pain
I'm exorcizing my demons
and understanding
my pains deeper meaning

The Book of Born Free - Volume One

(Jewel #151)
read "**Blueprint for Black Power**"
by Amos Wilson
he knows how to **Awaken the Natural Genius of Black Children**
Baba Wilson
gives us a clear path to victory
cuz when you learn from your history
your future isn't a mystery

(Jewel #152)
read "**Economic Democracy**"
by J.W. Smith
apply it to your community
mend the financial rift
he shows how whites maintain
the economic power structure
he gives us the architecture
on how to keep wealth within your culture

(Jewel #153)
read "**Yurugu**"
by Marimba Ani
she breaks down the original philosophy
of white supremacy
Mama Ani intellectually
lays out a cultural connection
for the African social
and spiritual resurrection

The Book of Born Free - Volume One

(Jewel #154)
read "**The Activist's Handbook**"
by Randy Shaw
hit the streets
and challenge unjust laws
his book gives you
a great foundation
on how to create and maintain
strong grassroots formations

(Jewel #155)
read whatever spiritual book
that moves you deep in your heart
cuz without a belief in God
we're dead from the start
but don't judge your neighbor
if they pray in a different way
we have no time
to bang over bibles today

The Book of Born Free - Volume One

(Jewel #156)
we survived the storm
but don't take it for granted
families without a plan
will be swept off the planet
build with your people
write your ideas down
you can debate and celebrate
after you've found higher ground

(Jewel #157)
study your environment
have an off-the-road mentality
in times of catastrophe
it can help you keep your sanity
practice walking through the woods
learn every back road and trail
refuse to fail
and your family will prevail

(Jewel #158)
you need food bars, water, medicines
flashlights and candles
a radio, a weapon
and a Rambo knife with the hunting apparel
purification tablets, toilet paper
and more than one waterproof match
you need to learn how to kill and prepare
all the food you catch

The Book of Born Free - Volume One

(Jewel #159)
don't just use your spiritual lessons
to sing and praise
study scriptures
to see how those nations were saved
and I don't mean saved
from hell fire after you die
learn how they physically survived
and left those hard times behind

(Jewel #160)
learn how to listen to others
follow clear instructions
you can minimize disruptions
when you understand the function
each person own your office
everyone else follow suit
when disasters hit
there's no time for petty disputes

The Book of Born Free - Volume One

(Jewel #161)
do you believe in global warming
is this weather is the norm
no matter what you believe
you can't brush off a 1,000-mile storm
the climate is changing
denial is death
fortify your nest
for the day the sun rises in the west

(Jewel 162)
within 48 hours
New York City went down
they never thought you could drown
in the middle of midtown
with all its technology
and advanced metropolitan life
they would give it all up
for food and a warm place to spend the night

(Jewel #163)
where's your diagram
where's your design
where's your program
where's your outline
whether its weather
or war
how will you and yours
be secured and endure

The Book of Born Free - Volume One

(Jewel #164)
warm winters
frosty spring
are you ready for what man
and nature will bring
have you been training
have you been planning
knowledge is worthless
without a clear understanding

(Jewel #165)
have you made
any new alliances
have you merged your farmers
with your scientists
if disaster hit
who will come to your aid
I pray that you've done more
than throw shade and get paid

The Book of Born Free - Volume One

(Jewel #166)
Cosby's betrayal is stunning
and profound
his actions must be denounced
smash all idols to the ground
his final epitaph will read comedian
father figure, and serial rapist
it's always the ones who act the most self-righteous
who are always the most heinous

(Jewel #167)
why can't we collectively
love our daughters
why can't we collectively
protect our daughters
why can't we collectively
support our daughters
why can't we collectively
believe our daughters

(Jewel #168)
I was a Cosby kid
my daughter was a Cosby kid
we tried to close our eyelids
we didn't want to accept what he did
he had the gall to call out black kid's culpability
condemn them for their irresponsibility
when it was his immoral activities
that exceeded all civilized acceptability

The Book of Born Free - Volume One

(Jewel #169)
the Illuminati didn't take down Cosby
he picked his own cross
he chose to slow dance with the devil
and paid a heavy cost
Bill willingly jumped into the trap
and did a handstand in quicksand
don't blame the convenient bogeyman
for the evil choices of man

(Jewel #170)
I agree with the disclaimer
in front of Cosby's art exhibits
but will they put a disclaimer
on Polanski's movie tickets
what about the cinematic work
of Spacey, Weinstein, and Collins
if they don't get a disclaimer
it's a mother fucking problem

The Book of Born Free - Volume One

(Jewel #171)
America celebrates Robert E Lee
but not Colin Kaepernick
America commemorates Stonewall Jackson
but not Colin Kaepernick
America acknowledges Nathan Forrest
but not Colin Kaepernick
America pays homage to Samuel Cox
but not Colin Kaepernick

(Jewel #172)
America shows deference to Jefferson Davis
but not Colin Kaepernick
America shows reverence to Alex Stephens
but not Colin Kaepernick
America memorializes Leonidas K. Polk
but not Colin Kaepernick
America recognizes P. G. T. Beauregard
but not Colin Kaepernick

(Jewel #173)
America calls Patrick Henry patriotic
but not Colin Kaepernick
America thinks Henry Knox is iconic
but not Colin Kaepernick
America gives The Boston Tea Party praise
but not Colin Kaepernick
America gives Bill Molineux accolades
but not Colin Kaepernick

The Book of Born Free - Volume One

(Jewel #174)
Ray Lewis put Kaepernick in a seat
because of his girlfriend's tweet
that's so weak, have you forgotten
those 2 dead bodies in the street
Ray Lewis lied to the police
the Ravens didn't have him released
now they want to white-ball Kaep
because he challenged the beast

(Jewel #175)
we already let Tommie Smith
and John Carlos down
instead of freedom's crown
we let them be swallowed up in the ground
now they're giving Kaep the boot
to leave him financially destitute
do we have the collective balls
to give him a golden parachute

The Book of Born Free - Volume One

(Jewel #176)
they want Beyoncé safe and sexy
not sober and serious
telling black women to get into formation
has the white media furious
they say she defiled the Super Bowl
they wanna take back the bankroll
it burns deep in their souls
when we move outside of their control

(Jewel #177)
it was all good a week ago
until B started mixing Creoles with Negros
now these assholes
want to put Lye in Blue Ivy's afro
Tabasco in her Dereon bag
Chi-Raq Panther swag
why does loving ourselves
make them so damn mad

(Jewel #178)
I drank the lemonade
and now I'm refreshed
blessed
even Jay got some personal shit off his chest
Lemonade is a popular drink
and it still is
whether it's hers or his
looking within is an investment in your kids

The Book of Born Free - Volume One

(Jewel #179)
is this how
American diversity works
Solange can't be black
at the Kraftwerk concert
these white jerks hate when we enjoy
our beautiful blackness
I guess we can be black in skin color
but not in open practice

(Jewel #180)
many whites love our black skin
they love the way we shine
they love our unique style
they love the way we rhyme
but they don't love our black mind
or black independence
conservative or liberal
their existence is based on our dependence

The Book of Born Free - Volume One

(Jewel #181)
I love and honor
all our beloved figures hidden
centuries of African history
has been remixed and rewritten
we've only seen a piece
we've only had a taste
we need to destroy the system
that hid them in the first damn place

(Jewel #182)
some drop lyrical bombs
others throw institutional grenades
Texas wants to take the word slave
out of their triangular trades
they know that dropping the word slave
will distort the history, empathy, and sentiment
so can we call the Holocaust
a Lemony Snicket Series of Unfortunate Events

(Jewel #183)
the next time you show me a video
of young black's flash mobbin in a mall
I'll show you young white Football Hooligans
in a bloodthirsty street brawl
when young black's wild out
we ALL get called out
but when young whites dumb out
the media crickets come out

The Book of Born Free - Volume One

(Jewel #184)
when you see an older white woman
gently stirring her tea
grab your gun and pray
that the lord thy God is with thee
don't answer any questions
take a different TSA route
smash that fuckin teacup
and GET OUT!

(Jewel #185)
I hate having to analyze
so many things in terms of race
but things are hard to ignore
when they're right in your face
on the surface things look like
they're improving at a turtles rate
but when you scratch off the new paint
you'll see and smell the old racism and hate

The Book of Born Free - Volume One

(Jewel #186)
don't ever take away
a man's reason to live
don't threaten his home
his money, his wife, or his kids
cuz once all his riches, land, dignity, and love
is taken away
he'll become a force of destruction and death
for the rest of his days

(Jewel #187)
hunger
is a vicious distraction
it sets in motion
a hellish chain reaction
and even though we don't live by bread alone
please don't deny it
cuz an empty belly
is the precursor for all bloody riots

(Jewel #188)
morality doesn't magically come
from mediating on the good news
this jewel is just a clue
you must be able to take care of you
when humans are denied basic
food, clothing, and shelter
right and wrong gets murdered
by the new religion of Helter Skelter

The Book of Born Free - Volume One

(Jewel #189)
why should our children listen
if we're not building a future for them
verbal gems won't distract them
from embracing American sins
we're a nation within a nation
searching for a nationality
Dr. Clarke warned that we could lose our family
if we choose this insanity

(Jewel #190)
if you want to help stop the violence
feed the people
manufactured poverty is evil
come out the churches and cathedrals
no one wants to hear a sermon
when their belly is burning
abandonment is the current lesson
our children are learning

The Book of Born Free - Volume One

(Jewel #191)
some say my temperature is too cold
others say it's too hot
I say never mind as long as my
pledges and oaths are not forgot
for if I submit to their definitions
I submit to their dominance
and my once bright future
will portend a vision more ominous

(Jewel #192)
let's be done with long-winded speeches
and brimstone sermons
let the fruit of thy labor
be the standard to determine
standing at a podium
causes many to overstate their grace
their radiant smiles hide a debased heart
filled with empty space

(Jewel #193)
applause has killed more than a million plagues
shot from a million cannons
the sound distorts the line
between God and Mammon
you become a contemptible shell
yelling about me and me alone
arrogance tries to make a royal home
on top a valley of dry brittle bones

The Book of Born Free - Volume One

(Jewel #194)
only the dead
desire war
only the dead lust for and adore
innocent blood on the floor
don't follow these lost corpses
back to their grave
don't get caught up in the wave
of shadowy images in Plato's cave

(Jewel #195)
what real power have we achieved
what real power have we seen
do we control one vaccine
what real power do we have in this machine
why do we still have to say please
where are our house keys
why can't we see that our brilliant black president
was just another Lady Eloise

The Book of Born Free - Volume One

(Jewel #196)
white nations didn't become wealthy
because they read Adam Smith
they became wealthy
because they had mafias, cartels, and syndicates
they created Ivy League schools
like Princeton, Yale, and MIT
to justify and rationalize
the atrocities of white supremacy

(Jewel #197)
color might not matter
in the highest realms of spirituality
but socially, financially, and politically
you better deal with the reality
white people control too many
life sustaining resources on this planet
before we can topple it
we need to confront it and understand it

(Jewel #198)
America let the Ku Klux Klan
exist and recruit for 150 years
America let the Ku Klux Klan
terrorize and murder for 150 years
America let the Ku Klux Klan
buy land and guns for 150 years
America will let the Ku Klux Klan
flourish for another 150 years

The Book of Born Free - Volume One

(Jewel #199)
they say slavery's over
but don't do a crime
the 13th Amendment
will get you every time
if that doesn't get you
structured poverty will
crime follows those
who can't legally pay their bills

(Jewel #200)
when was America GREAT
and I'm not being facetious
by a show of hands
who really believes this
GREAT means excellent, remarkable
and extremely extraordinary
racially, when has America
ever fit that definition in the dictionary

The Book of Born Free - Volume One
<u>Keep the Pressure On</u>
(a song waiting 2 be sung - 2001)

they steal elections
don't let them steal your voice
they tell us to vote
but they ignore our choice
they say we're free
but not enough to say no
they call us un-american
when we don't go with the flow
but

keep the pressure on
keep hitting the streets
keep fighting back
never retreat
keep the pressure on
keep speaking your mind
our children's lives
are on the line

the Patriot Act
is unpatriotic
the mass media is
a deadly narcotic
they push lies into our minds
like dope in our veins
they control our souls
with pleasure and pain

The Book of Born Free - Volume One

they tell us one thing
then they do another
but the time is right
to pull back the covers
so,

keep the pressure on
keep hitting the streets
keep fighting back
never retreat
keep the pressure on
keep speaking your mind
our children's lives
are on the line

go to your church
go to your mosque
tell the people
the wars must stop
go to your synagogue
go on your rooftop
tell the people
the wars must stop
go home to your families
go out on your block
tell the people
the wars must stop
go into the light
go into the darkest spot
tell the people
the wars must stop

The Book of Born Free - Volume One

cuz, they tell us one thing
then they do another
but the time is right
to pull back the covers
so,

keep the pressure on
keep hitting the streets
keep fighting back
never retreat
keep the pressure on
keep speaking your mind
our children's lives
are on the line

Born Free #therealbornfree

The Book of Born Free - Volume One

(Jewel #201)
on November 8th, 2016
I heard millions of sinister orgasmic screams
as Donald J Trump
took the reins of the American regime
the ALT-Right and the ALT-Left
proudly poked out their chest
pledged to build a new eagle's nest
on the backs of the oppressed

(Jewel #202)
remember this dark moment
remember this inauguration
remember who stood with God
and who stood with Satan
remember who kissed the ring
remember who bowed in the tower
remember all the plagues released
by this un-peaceful transfer of power

(Jewel #203)
it's ironic that there's a so-called attack
on fake news
when it was fake history and fake religion
that mis-educated me and you
fake amendments, fake integration
and a fake justice system
that made real slaves, real poverty
and very real victims

The Book of Born Free - Volume One

(Jewel #204)
if you want to perform for Trump
go bend over and perform
conform
but I can't co-sign that racist platform
I've sworn my allegiance
to the Heavenly Father of Jesus
and I won't stand in agreement
with a demon for financial convenience

(Jewel #205)
Trump doesn't have the power
to bring about the last days
that's a power
that only God can display
Trump's just a mortal man
delicate bones, and orange flesh
take a deep breath
we're going to pass this test

The Book of Born Free - Volume One

(Jewel #206)
white America don't ever let me hear you
call a rapper a misogynist
when you picked a racist pussy grabber
to be your president
assault in his locker room
while they de-fund Planned Parenthood
your stupid hatred of me
fucked yourself over real good

(Jewel #207)
America didn't change
old furniture got rearranged
new paint on the walls
they launched new campaigns
white supremacy got stronger
its tentacles got longer
if you believe these warmongers
you've been conquered

(Jewel #208)
Muslim's are being banned
but the ALT-Right freely roam
the KKK are the police
and sexual predators call the white house home
this is Resident Evil
the newest chapter
our ancestors warned
that you can't reform captors and slave masters

The Book of Born Free - Volume One

(Jewel #209)
while we're fucking around
they're fracking the ground
only fools believe money
makes the world go around
without infrastructure
you're just a loud-mouth mother fucker
and the world sees you as a sucker
cuz you dance and rap for your supper

(Jewel #210)
ever since Trump won
our internal beefs have escalated
the gross stupidity of this
can't be overstated
we say we understand the plan
we say we can see through the plot
yet those who hate unified
and those who love have not

The Book of Born Free - Volume One

(Jewel #211)
you can't pass freedom down
from generation to generation
each generation
must take and maintain their own liberation
no matter how much you bend over
and pay for your lubrication
political preachers can't guarantee
personal or economic salvation

(Jewel #212)
with all the money and power
that we boast to skyrocket
how many policy makers
do we have in our pocket
who are the puppets that dance
for our benefit
we might be deeply in it
but we really don't get it

(Jewel #213)
seven hundred and eighty-seven billion
was the bailout stimulus bill
who's bailing out those going to Canada
to get their prescriptions filled
corporations claim large sums are necessary
to restructure their teams
but when black women needed bailouts
they got called lazy welfare queens

The Book of Born Free - Volume One

(Jewel #214)
I respect the reparations movement
but it is pointless
begging and begging
will only lead to flaccid disappointment
reparations is not about getting a barrel of cash
for one little home
reparations is about turning your whole village
into a separate and independent empowerment zone

(Jewel #215)
The Freedom Act is the Patriot Act
The Patriot Act is the Freedom Act
no matter what they call it
we're still under surveillance and attack
under the guise of tracking down
terrorist cells and spies
they'll catalog, categorize
and criminalize all our lives

The Book of Born Free - Volume One

(Jewel #216)
this American horror story
has us walking among the tombstones
living and dying
between the ringtones on a cell phone
Snapchat
niggerized apps
clickbait self-hate
and aristocrat doormats

(Jewel #217)
we chose Madea over Nat Turner
Barabbas over Jesus
fame over freedom
dreaming over leaving
complaining over doing
voting over building
the results of our choices
have been disappointing and chilling

(Jewel #218)
has there ever been a travel ban
on the Ku Klux Klan
has any president ever put them under
an executive plan
are they on any terror watch list
are they even considered terrorists
no matter what you hope or wish
it's time to physically resist

The Book of Born Free - Volume One

(Jewel #219)
I'm not proud
of that ragged old flag
they used that ragged old flag
to hang my great grand mom and dad
that ragged old flag was embroidered
on old Jim Crow bags
so I don't care if you're mad
but I can't love that ragged old flag

(Jewel #220)
all black everything, black skin
black kids, a black library card
black love, black bride
and you know I got black God
black rage, black history
with the deep black blues
black nation, black news
the original black Jews

The Book of Born Free - Volume One

(Jewel #221)
an enemy of your enemy
is still not your friend
don't let the new alliance bring compliance
because people pretend
pay close attention
don't let warning signs
go unheeded
don't let your lust for victory
leave you manipulated and defeated

(Jewel #222)
beware of the people
who follow rules without thought
they're the ones who are
easily seduced and bought
they'll sell you out without hesitation
or a moment of lost sleep
be extremely careful
of the company you keep

(Jewel #223)
death comes to us all
it doesn't need to be expedited
death will eventually show up
it doesn't need to be invited
your life is a Godly gift
don't recklessly put it in harm's way
cuz you don't want death to show up early today
with your final bouquet

The Book of Born Free - Volume One

(Jewel #224)
if you allow your foe to know
all that you've been planning
you'll ensure your enemy
will be the last one standing
choose discretion over bravado
learn how to use the truth and the lie
in this game of thrones
you either win or you die

(Jewel #225)
I don't believe in going to war
for the sake of going to war
but I do believe in the peace
that lives on the other side of war
an eye for an eye way of thinking
can lead to generations of bloodshed
but too much talking
can lead to your extinction instead

The Book of Born Free - Volume One

(Jewel #226)
indifference pollutes the blood
cowardice turns men into mud
greed increases the speed
and horror of the flood
evil's greatest ally
is a man who can idly stand by
and watch with a disconnected eye
as his fellow man withers and dies

(Jewel #227)
slavery is swift and changeable
it will never be static
you can be locked in chains
or hooked as an addict
you can be enslaved mentally
or it can represent itself as debt
but make no mistake about it
slavery is still in effect

(Jewel #228)
untie your truth
from the fearful tether of scorn
leave it as it was
on the day it was born
leave it unvarnished
and in its original state
let its nudity and virginity
dictate its fate

The Book of Born Free - Volume One

(Jewel #229)
it's as much post racial
as its post anti-Semitic
post sexist
and post homophobic
post terrorism
and post classism
these erroneous dictums
are a part of the new millennium prisons

(Jewel #230)
even our most eloquent and eminent
are scared and hesitant
to stand up and kill
this degenerate elephant
we ignore all the evidence
and sacrifice our intelligence
just to sit at the table
and choke on this elegant excrement

The Book of Born Free - Volume One

(Jewel #231)
the stop snitchin campaign
is a complete fool's move
civilians shouldn't have to abide
by gang rules
if you're a real gangsta nigga
you shouldn't be afraid of jail
and if you are
get off the corner and put down the fish scale

(Jewel #232)
I support stop snitching
if you're working like Chairman Fred
and you're counteracting the oppression
put on us by the Feds
but if you just want to be a nigga on the block
terrorizing Mrs. Ruby
turning your ass in
is my revolutionary duty

(Jewel #233)
black people didn't start
the stop snitching conversation
I think it was started
at the police station
no, I think it was started
at the Vatican
or maybe when Columbus released pathogens
on indigenous Americans

The Book of Born Free - Volume One

(Jewel #234)
I don't make excuses for losers
or cover up the stupidity
don't label me an angry black man
filled with blind hatred or insecurity
I'm just trying to stop us
from falling back into the bottomless pit
and I don't think we can transcend race
by ignoring or denying it

(Jewel #235)
I'm not a black supremacist
nor do I over romanticize the past
I'm not trying' to pass the buck
on why we haven't surpassed
I don't blame the white man
for every drop of acid rain
but killing the devil in the room
might help ease our pain

The Book of Born Free - Volume One

(Jewel #236)
it's funny that we call it the trap
cuz it's literally a motherfuckin trap!
and the only ones getting caught and clapped
are young blacks
who needs Cointelpro, police terrorism
and The Patriot Act
now that it's profitable to rap and stack
about this black death trap

(Jewel #237)
black teens are killing
and dying way too often
no money for the kids
but they put suicide doors on his coffin
a collective death wish
with a Louie Vuitton twist
criminally blinded
by a dumbed down rappers frozen wrist

(Jewel #238)
listen, if you gotta be a nigga
then be a field nigga
and if you can't be that nigga
then shut the fuck up nigga!
and you can't stop niggas from saying nigga
by burying it six feet deep
the only way is to re-educate and love those niggas
who are still fast asleep

The Book of Born Free - Volume One

(Jewel #239)
these cops are acquitted
because they don't see killing us as a crime
they get away with it
because we're in nigga state of mind
if you really want to honor Sean Bell
his family, and his memory
love yourself, love your neighbor
and clean up your fuckin community

(Jewel #240)
all these so-called conscious scholars beefing
fake supreme chieftains
they're Legion
dick size contests at the feed the people meeting
ego over reason
distraction is a form of treason
they don't care who they're misleadin'
just as long as they're eaten

The Book of Born Free - Volume One

(Jewel #241)
we're killing each other
on the mic
we're killing each other
in real life
we're killing each other despite
our belief in Muhammad and Christ
we're killing each other no matter
if our children our sacrificed

(Jewel #242)
we're killing each other
because Willie Lynch was successful
we're killing each other
because poverty is stressful
we're killing each other
because of a lack of proper education
we're killing each other
because we no longer believe in our salvation

(Jewel #243)
we're killing each other
because we've become cowards
we're killing each other
because we've submitted to white power
we're killing each other
because we've given up
we're killing each other
because we won't step the fuck up!

The Book of Born Free - Volume One

(Jewel #244)
we're killing each other
because we've forgotten God lives within
we're killing each other
because we're afraid of powerful white men
we're killing each other
because we took the racists bait
we're killing each other
because we're infected with self-hate

(Jewel #245)
we're killing each other
because they infested us with crack
we're killing each other
because the constitution stabbed us in the back
we're killing each other
because they created the projects and the trap
we're killing each other
because we fell in love with both traps

The Book of Born Free - Volume One

(Jewel #246)
we're killing each other
while Trump tries to take our rights
we're killing each other
while the Klan walks around in plain sight
we're killing each other
while the flood waters rise
we're killing each other
while the universal healthcare bill dies

(Jewel #247)
we're killing each other
because we don't think as a nation
we're killing each other
because we believe in fake integration
we're killing each other
because we're waiting to be saved
we're killing each other
because we've stopped being brave

(Jewel #248)
we're killing each other
because we're afraid to kill our oppressors
we're killing each other
because we believe we're lesser
we're killing each other
because of our love affair with the streets
we're killing each other
because we've become so weak

The Book of Born Free - Volume One

(Jewel #249)
we're killing each other
because of 400 years of oppression
we're killing each other
because we fell for the deception
we're killing each other
because of self-doubt
we're killing each other
because our leaders sold us out

(Jewel #250)
we're killing each other
because of mass unemployment
we're killing each other
because of mass disappointment
we're killing each other
because we didn't build an infrastructure
we're killing each other
because we fell in love with our abductor

The Book of Born Free - Volume One

(Jewel #251)
we're killing each other
because our bond is broken with black women
we're killing each other
because of unhealthy foods in our kitchens
we're killing each other
because our bond is broken with black men
we're killing each other
because we make more enemies than friends

(Jewel #252)
we're killing each other
because we're deaf, dumb, and blind
we're killing each other
because we're trapped online
we're killing each other
because we lack Knowledge of Self
we're killing each other
because we confused money with wealth

(Jewel #253)
we're killing each other
because we won't help ourselves
we're killing each other
because of the wrong books on our shelves
we're killing each other
because we've embraced the racist stereotype
we're killing each other
because we think and act like racist whites

The Book of Born Free - Volume One

(Jewel #254)
we're killing each other
because we're choosing to be niggers
we're killing each other
because we're scared to think bigger
we're killing each other
because we're running from our past
we're killing each other
because we're trapped by the past

(Jewel #255)
but no matter why
we're killing each other
WE HAVE TO
STOP KILLING EACH OTHER
it's critical and imperative
that we change this hateful narrative
forgive, and show our children
the right way to LOVE and LIFE

The Book of Born Free - Volume One

(Jewel #256)
black women started
Black Lives Matter and that matters
so don't come at her
in a disrespectful manner
black women have always had our back
front, and sides
so when they're vilified and denied
brothers we gotta ride

(Jewel #257)
there's a difference between
black lives matter and white lives matter
study the history
queue up the data
black people are marching
for equality and solidarity
white people are marching
for total superiority over all humanity

(Jewel #258)
if white money is funding
our Black Lives Matter crusade
black and brown communities
will face a serious blockade
when whites invest their money
they expect to own and control the table
the combination of white money and black power
has always been a heartbreaking and fatal

The Book of Born Free - Volume One

(Jewel #259)
if Black Lives Matter is going to be
our main defender
it must have an
unapologetic black nationalistic agenda
it can't kindly negotiate
our slate and fate
it must dictate, dominate
and dismantle this police state

(Jewel #260)
if Black Lives Don't Matter
to black people
we'll NEVER kill this extremely beatable
American eagle
the us killing us murders
in New Orleans, Chicago, and Baltimore
are literally stopping us
from winning this winnable war

The Book of Born Free - Volume One

(Jewel #261)
some niggas will get to Paris
and live all lavish
go couture clothes shopping
in a horse drawn carriage
but most will be trapped back on the block
all depressed and ravaged
unchallenged and spiritually famished
tryin not to become the next cannibalistic savage

(Jewel #262)
if you want your seeds to read
pick up a book FIRST
teach them that history is best qualified
to reward all research
knowledge is the foundation
wisdom is the communication
understanding the situation
will help keep them off the plantation

(Jewel #263)
what's better than 2 billionaires
LAND!
shake your deeds
if you really understand
real money talk isn't about money
profits or losses
real bosses control natural resources
and formless military forces

The Book of Born Free - Volume One

(Jewel #264)
I don't give a fuck if Russia
hacked the American election
I care about how America hacked
into our African perception
they changed our OS
the malware made us unaware victims
this nigga virus made us fight each other
to stay in this prison

(Jewel #265)
I'm not a race baiter, slave traitor
or mainstream hater
I'm more like the Alpha and Omega
mixed with a little Darth Vader
a greater great debater
lost-found vindicator
a godly creator that travels beyond
the magnetic equator

The Book of Born Free - Volume One

(Jewel #266)
I don't celebrate the 4th
because we're NOT independent
you DON'T gain independence
through amendments
independence is ownership of land
supplying your own demands
why would I celebrate the death of my ancestors
by my enemy's hands

(Jewel #267)
when you invoke the spirit of the Pilgrims
you release the Pogrom
you unwittingly endorse the past and present
Maafa and maelstrom
don't let them use
the sanctity of family and charity
to hide a vicious legacy
of genocide and barbarity

(Jewel #268)
create your own holidays
your own sacred rituals
honor your own intellectuals
and creative individuals
don't get mad or jealous
at other cultural parades
just raise your children to love and appreciate
the special days you made

The Book of Born Free - Volume One

(Jewel #269)
I love Umoja Karamu
and Kwanzaa
every single year
it's a huge extravaganza
family, love, and good food
set the joyous mood
and after celebrating my culture
my whole being is renewed

(Jewel #270)
I don't work on January 1st
or January 15
on February 4th
I say mother fuck this racist machine
on May 19th
and June 19th
I'm plotting underneath
to give lady "liberty" her final wreath

The Book of Born Free - Volume One

(Jewel #271)
Cecil John Rhodes was one of the world's
sickest white supremacist
yet you named your highest scholarship
after this brutal sadomasochist
it's unfathomable and typical
that you honor this genocidal killer
can you imagine a college fund
named after Bin Laden or Hitler

(Jewel #272)
that monster Rhodes made me think about
that butcher King Leopold
and how that devil murdered
my people all throughout the Congo
he mutilated men, women
and little children
he's one of white supremacy's
favorite hero villains

(Jewel #273)
we were taught to embrace Lincoln, Kennedy
Clinton and the like
we were taught reject
Garvey, X, and Farrakhan's light
our slave masters became our gods
and our gods became our devils
we'll never rise beyond this
level if continue to be our enemy's vessels

The Book of Born Free - Volume One

(Jewel #274)
you created Cointelpro
to find and kill the Black Messiah
you killed Martin, Malcolm, and Hampton
under a hail of gunfire
but you took all this truth
out of your-story books
then you lied and deified
all your enslavers, abusers, and crooks

(Jewel #275)
Trump is just the newest incarnation
of hatred and bigotry
I'm quite sure that his legacy
will be fixed in American history
instead of calling him a racist
they'll say he was a controversial figure
they'll 1984
all his tweets on Twitter

The Book of Born Free - Volume One

(Jewel #276)
you don't have to
beseech the Holy oracle
to know that Trump
and his supporters are deplorable
horrible
and intellectually incurable
their mentality resides
at the bottom of a urinal

(Jewel #277)
Donald Trump's a douche bag
this we've learned
but it's his constituents
that has me that most concerned
Trump's ignorance
would have no relevance
without a strong support system
helping him spread his pestilence

(Jewel #278)
rape culture is alive and well
in America today
Trump calls it locker room talk
trying to trivialize it away
reducing women to things, objects
and body parts
doesn't just speak to the man
it reveals his true heart

The Book of Born Free - Volume One

(Jewel #279)
here comes Donald Trump
speaking the new Mein Kampf
America, you can't front
this is exactly what you want
look at his electoral numbers
check all the media coverage
you might act like you're appalled
but I know you really love it

(Jewel #280)
Trump represent's
America unvarnished
raw sewage and carnage
the truth un-garnished
all his fear mongering
and bully rhetoric
appeals to the closet confederate
and well financed racial degenerate

The Book of Born Free - Volume One

(Jewel #281)
read Chomsky's
"Manufacturing Consent"
look at the true face
of your government
the choices you make
may not be your own
are you sure you're not
just a target marketed clone

(Jewel #282)
read, **"People's History of America"**
by Howard Zinn
look at history from the P.O.V.
of indigenous women and men
read and listen
to the other side of the coin
and think about that
when Uncle Satan asks you to join

(Jewel #283)
read, **"The Shock Doctrine"**
by Naomi Klein
understand how they
manipulated the times
read how they use shock therapy
socially and financially
study how they've mastered
the alchemy of catastrophe

The Book of Born Free - Volume One

(Jewel #284)
read, Amy Goodman's
"Exception to the Rulers"
study all the
real shakers and movers
learn who profits
from all these global conflicts and wars
she reveals this
and much-much more

(Jewel #285)
read anything
that you can get your hands on
read and read
from dusk to dawn
and after you finish reading
put your work boots on and do
because reading alone
WILL NOT SAVE YOU

The Book of Born Free - Volume One

(Jewel #286)
poor neighborhoods are created
with a stroke of the pen
redlining stops you
before you begin
don't believe that black people
didn't strive to get their own home
redlining was designed
to deny us proper loans

(Jewel #287)
when they started giving us loans
they called them subprime
our financial destruction
was written between the lines
the interest rates soared
higher than the golden sunshine
the foreclosure of our new homes
was just a matter of time

(Jewel #288)
we can't afford to be ignorant
of what's really going on
because we always end up singing
the same ole' song
so before you go back to sleep
let me give you a little information
a black president
is not the same as black liberation

The Book of Born Free - Volume One

(Jewel #289)
develop new skills
run new drills
get out of debt
pay your fuckin bills
have short and long-term goals
diversify your bankroll
and get your god damn appetite
under your control

(Jewel #290)
snap out of the fantasy
about how you want the world to run
voting, saving pennies
and social security under the Florida sun
this government is not your government
hard but true
stop waiting around
for them to remember to rescue you

The Book of Born Free - Volume One

(Jewel #291)
power doesn't concede
to sentimentality
power doesn't care
about principality
power can only be checked
by the threat of more power
if you waver in this understanding
you will be devoured

(Jewel #292)
we have to move beyond
black faces in high places
we need a plan that takes us beyond
these political races
we need substance not ceremony
solutions not sound bites
there are more directions
than just left and right

(Jewel #293)
the Italians control Italy
the English control England
the Iranians control Iran
and the Japanese control Japan
the Chinese control China
and white Americans control America
so why is it militant to say
that black Africans should control Africa

The Book of Born Free - Volume One

(Jewel #294)
move the money
open an account today
move the money
don't hesitate or delay
the movement needs a black bank
to end postponed dreams
the movement needs
billions of independent revenue streams

(Jewel #295)
an underdeveloped human being
is the worst curse on earth
feed your babies knowledge
BEFORE the moment of their birth
don't wait until they fail
or end up in jail
before you show them love
and how to balance their scales

The Book of Born Free - Volume One

(Jewel #296)
don't try to normalize
or glamorize
that ratchet bullshit
that helps to stigmatize
they want to niggerize, polarize
and pulverize
us until we can't recognize God
love or the sunrise

(Jewel #297)
don't say the white man
until you've looked in the mirror FIRST!
don't talk about unseen hands
until you've looked in the mirror FIRST!
don't talk about the media
until you've looked in the mirror FIRST!
don't talk about Trump
until you've looked in the mirror FIRST!

(Jewel #298)
this nigga shit
is killing me
Hosea 4:6
is a prophesy
the atrocity
is our hypocrisy
you can't rape your sister
then complain about the lack of democracy

The Book of Born Free - Volume One

(Jewel #299)
one check of IG
one check of Snapchat
one check of Periscope
one check of all the apps
and you'll see the sad fact
that will put your head in your lap
these platforms are playgrounds
for young broken blacks

(Jewel #300)
one check of the churches
one check of the mosques
one check of the temples
one check of the synagogues
and you'll start to sob
when you hear the impotent narcissistic dialogue
coming from these old counterfeit
ignorant black demagogues

The Book of Born Free - Volume One

(Jewel #301)
they'll call you a snitch
if you reveal the dirt your neighbor did
but what if your neighbor is in the kitchen
cooking crack for kids
what if they turned your child
into their mule, runner, or client
would you still be so quiet
and ghetto compliant

(Jewel #302)
if you need a cop to sit at the top
of your block to feel safe
and you get your groceries
from behind a clear bulletproof case
your neighborhood has fallen deep
into the devil's embrace
and anyone who likes or glorifies
this sad state is a damn disgrace

(Jewel #303)
once the stereotype becomes true
the end is dangerously near
while you laugh and cheer
your true self slowly disappears
the stereotypes that you think are funny
are ultimately grotesque
and the more they're expressed
the longer we'll be oppressed

The Book of Born Free - Volume One

(Jewel #304)
the main reason our kids
are being laid down and locked up
is because too many of us grown ass men
won't step the fuck up
and just like Malcolm said
"we're afraid to bleed"
but more importantly
we're afraid to lead

(Jewel #305)
it's time to talk about God
BEFORE the next school shootin'
face our addictions
BEFORE the death of the next Whitney Houston
talk to your children
BEFORE the next group of flash mobs
and pool our money together
BEFORE the next wave of lost jobs

The Book of Born Free - Volume One

(Jewel #306)
lying to yourself
is the thinnest of veils
truth and justice
will always prevail
peace of mind is greater
than a piece of the pie
everything the devil has told you
is a LIE!

(Jewel #307)
I speak the truth
and only the truth
I played Dr. Ben and Clarke tapes
inside the voting booth
a lot of Francis Cress
to decipher this mess
they all teach that voting
gave us the illusion of progress

(Jewel #308)
I'm not angry
but I can be
I'm not violent
but I can be
I'm appropriate
I'll be whatever I need to be
everything depends on how much
you love me or hurt me

The Book of Born Free - Volume One

(Jewel #309)
3 strikes and you're out
1 strike and you're out
this is what
the Clintons are all about
3 strikes and you're out
1 strike and you're out
this is what
America is all about

(Jewel #310)
we're more famous than fortunate
more rich than wealthy
more trained than educated
more fed than healthy
more rappers than emcees
more strangers than neighbors
more unchained than free
and more sheep than saviors

The Book of Born Free - Volume One

(Jewel #311)
when we get understandably angry
they stop us in our tracks
justifiable anger
isn't afforded to blacks
we must always be deathly calm
and unrealistically amenable
foolishly reassuring
and treasonously commendable

(Jewel #312)
why can't we get
just as mad as you get
why can't we beat the drums of war
and sound conflicts trumpet
why do we have to smile
even when the wounds are bloody and fresh
why can't we do what you do
and avenge our loved ones death

(Jewel #313)
when white America gets bombed
she bombs back
when white America gets attacked
she attacks back
when white America feels threatened
she doesn't hesitate
but we're only allowed the weapons
of voting and debate to retaliate

The Book of Born Free - Volume One

(Jewel #314)
Israel wasn't considered militant
for pressuring Obama to bomb Iran
why didn't we tell Benjamin Netanyahu
to sing songs and hold hands
why don't we remind them
that two wrongs don't make a right
why don't we say that peaceful protesting
is the only right way to fight

(Jewel #315)
why are we so afraid
to confront this aging beast
fighting back
isn't a contradiction to peace
if we really believe in God
like we say we do
then we should know for a fact
that he'll see us through

The Book of Born Free - Volume One

(Jewel #316)
now that Justine Ruszczyk
has been murdered by Officer Noor
America can no longer ignore
or endure killer cops anymore
mayor Hodges is "heartsick" "frustrated"
"deeply disturbed"
it's rare to hear official empathetic words
when we're dead on the curb

(Jewel #317)
has anyone in the media
even slightly insinuated
that Justine's actions
should be carefully investigated
did she make the loud noise
did she make the wrong steps
or does her whiteness prevent her
from being blamed for her own tragic death

(Jewel #318)
every cop
isn't filthy and dirty
every cop
isn't my mortal enemy
but when those devil cops
murder, maim, and malign
all those so-called Serpico's
turn their backs and toe the fuckin line

The Book of Born Free - Volume One

(Jewel #319)
I went numb after seeing Yanez
murder Philando Castile
then the faith shattering acquittal
just sealed the deal
I'm not going to conceal
or hide how I feel
take them with you
is my final appeal

(Jewel #320)
I've got cops in my family
and I love them deeply
but I won't let you use
that love to defeat me
my unconditional love for them
doesn't make me pretend
that every person with a badge
is my protector or friend

The Book of Born Free - Volume One

(Jewel #321)
if you're white and you want to help
this black movement
sabotage the system of enslavement
and prove it
stand in front of me
when the bullets start spraying
give your life to prove
all the loyalty you're claiming

(Jewel #322)
some black and white people
misunderstand my thesis
they believe that I've come
to rip both races to pieces
but that's far from the truth
I've come to reveal and heal
I just don't give a fuck
about mass appeal

(Jewel #323)
reading books is not acting white
selling crack is not acting black
stereotypes like that
are some of the things holding us back
they love when we fall for the bait
choose self-hate and perpetuate
an ignorant mind state
that they love to broadcast and illustrate

The Book of Born Free - Volume One

(Jewel #324)
the color of your face
doesn't make you a part of your race
your position is based
on the consciousness that you embrace
snakes, traitors, and inform
ants come in all shapes and shades
your true color
emerges in what you're willing to do to get paid

(Jewel #325)
I have strong allies
in every nationality and hue
some of my allies
are inside your crew
but if any of my allies
are double agents
not even Almighty God can stop
my repayment

The Book of Born Free - Volume One

(Jewel #326)
fuck Trump's first 100 days;
I'm focused on our first 400 years
and why we're still here
crying the same tears with the same fears
Trump is pro-business
pro white supremacy
what weaponry have we built internally
to stop this racist hegemony

(Jewel #327)
the media doesn't hate Trump
the media made Trump
they gave his campaign a jump
he gave their ratings a bump
all this contrived controversy
is the fakest of the fake
and overlooking Pence
is a big mistake

(Jewel #328)
Obama said, the U.S. wants a partnership
with Africa and not charity
politics and politicians remind me
of a Mad Magazine parody
it's true that Africa's been dependent
since before we've been alive
but do you know about
the **Berlin Conference** of 1884-85

The Book of Born Free - Volume One

(Jewel #329)
Kathy Griffin got crazy and deep
she earned the hot seat
but I remember when they depicted Obama
as a monkey shot dead in the street
the NY Post said it was satire
quoted the 1st amendment
I guess you can artistically kill the president
when he's an African descendant

(Jewel #330)
Otto Warmbier goes into a coma in Korea
comes home and dies
the world calls North Korea's reason
complete bullshit and lies
Sandra Bland gets locked up
and suddenly dies
the world tells us not to over analyze
cuz it's just a simple "suicide"

The Book of Born Free - Volume One

(Jewel #331)
loving this machine
has us living in dangerous dream
we auction and barter
away our self-esteem
we demand nothing for our
votes and allegiance
and without cohesion
we can't hold them to their promises or agreements

(Jewel #332)
working together
is no longer an option
we can't afford to follow
these anti-black doctrines
we're down on the ground
where the rubber meets the road
either we get into nation mode
or prepare for the new barcode

(Jewel #333)
judge **Mark Ciavarella** got locked up
for sending kids to jail for kickbacks
this isn't a conspiracy theory
it's pure actual-facts
this is what happens when you
privatize the prison industrial complex
you turn all our children
into living contracts and checks

The Book of Born Free - Volume One

(Jewel #334)
republicans want to repeal and replace
to further kill and erase
none of us are safe
hear me NONE OF US ARE SAFE
I declare that if we don't find a way
to cover our own healthcare
no amount of protest or prayer
will protect us from legislative warfare

(Jewel #335)
Trumps tweets might make you nauseous
but he's not beneath the office
this is the same lawless office
that enslaved us and offed us
they filled coffin after coffin
with our people and prophets
please-please stop it
that office is sadistic and psychotic

The Book of Born Free - Volume One

(Jewel #336)
we need vocations
and scholarships
we need to know the difference
between good jobs and sole ownership
teach your children that having money is good
but legacy wealth is better
and that love, trust, and integrity
holds the whole thing together

(Jewel #337)
we need land ownership
without it we're screwed
we won't survive being dependent
on other nations for food
everything comes from the earth
we must acquire a major stake
cuz without it
we immediately lose control over our fate

(Jewel #338)
do I need to mention water
I hope I have your full attention
do you see what's going on
in Flint and Trenton
decades of lead in the pipes
toxic fluoride
if we don't get control of our own water supply
our cancer will continue multiply

The Book of Born Free - Volume One

(Jewel #339)
we must form our own gun clubs
and social institutions
master our own
internal distributions
set sky high standards
for human conduct and evolution
these are a few key ingredients
of a successful revolution

(Jewel #340)
if you think it is hot now
just wait until the shock of the hour
manufactured media powers
help the rise of prominent cowards
getting louder won't stop our children
from getting devoured
we need the clear word of God
and plenty of dry gunpowder

The Book of Born Free - Volume One

(Jewel #341)
I vomited
inside the voting booth
I felt like I was in
a coffin for the truth
take a sticker, smile
you did something significant
but when I pressed that green button
I felt defeated and impotent

(Jewel #342)
we can't leave a legacy
of militant submission
and black blood money
acquisitions
limp middle fingers
and yellow clinched fists
our children's-children-children
deserve better than this

(Jewel #343)
I hate that we depend
on the kindness of monsters
ignore God's prophets
and embrace obvious impostors
whenever a racist demagogue
uses a softer and gentler tone
immediately paint lamb's blood
on the doors of your home

The Book of Born Free - Volume One

(Jewel #344)
just sounding presidential
is completely inconsequential
ornamental
and poisonously detrimental
when devils assemble
they have many different rotten eggs to hatch
white supremacy isn't always
overtly savage in its attacks

(Jewel #345)
regardless of who sits in the white house
or who pulls the strings
The Most-High is the best knower
and reveler of all things
no earthly King, Queen
President or despot
can occupy or sit
in God's righteous spot

The Book of Born Free - Volume One

(Jewel #346)
Amos Wilson is my hero
Ella Baker is my hero
Martin Luther King is my hero
Marimba Ani is my hero
John Henrik Clarke is my hero
Ida B. Wells is my hero
Malcolm X is my hero
Sojourner Truth is my hero

(Jewel #347)
Harriet Tubman is my hero
W.E.B. Du Bois is my hero
Mary McLeod Bethune is my hero
Marcus Garvey is my hero
Shirley Chisholm is my hero
Yosef Ben-Jochannan is my hero
Francis Cress Welsing is my hero
Booker T. Washington is my hero

(Jewel #348)
Medgar Evers is my hero
bell hooks is my hero
Fredrick Douglass is my hero
Septima Poinsette Clark is my hero
Kwame Agyei Akoto is my hero
Assata Shakur is my hero
Cheikh Anta Diop is my hero
Angela Davis is my hero

The Book of Born Free - Volume One

(Jewel #349)
Prathia Hall is my hero
Louis Farrakhan is my hero
Coretta Scott King is my hero
Huey P. Newton is my hero
Betty Shabazz is my hero
Nelson Mandela is my hero
Winnie Mandela is my hero
Cornel West is my hero

(Jewel #350)
Elijah Muhammad is my hero
Dr. Dorothy Height is my hero
Fred Hampton is my hero
Fannie Lou Hamer is my hero
Chancellor Williams is my hero
Rosa Parks is my hero
Nat Turner is my hero
Pauline Ramsey is my hero

The Book of Born Free - Volume One

(Jewel #351)
how come we don't like any black leader
that America doesn't co-sign
no matter how valuable they are
we don't pay them any mind
we ignored the blueprints
of Wilson, Hare, Clarke and Ben
just so we don't irritate or offend
a few ignorant cracker-ass cracker white men

(Jewel #352)
old white men trying to control
a woman's sacred womb
you can't pass laws on Health Care
with no women in the room
no women at the table
no women on the board
our health will never be restored
with women being ignored

(Jewel #353)
I'm not hiding my blackness
under a digital bushel basket
I'm not digging my own grave
or building my own casket
my blackness isn't an intellectual exercise
or for casual sightseeing
it's the starting point
for getting to know me as a full human being

The Book of Born Free - Volume One

(Jewel #354)
a Trump presidency
doesn't scare me
I'm a child of God
so, cowardice would be hypocrisy
but in all honesty
I'm concerned about his future policies
his pro-rich philosophy
foreshadows a greater velocity for atrocities

(Jewel #355)
we must start
thinking as an emerging nation
this isn't about hate
or separating from all Caucasians
it's about providing food, clothing,
and shelter for over 35 million
it's about being responsible
for the natural welfare of our own children

The Book of Born Free - Volume One

(Jewel #356)
I don't have all the answers
I have more questions
no matter what's your impression
love is my intention
I'm speaking up
because we need an intervention
I expect many objections
but assimilation will never be my direction

(Jewel #357)
I don't believe
in partial freedom
I'm not interested
in a digital Garden of Eden
I'm not concerned with any new
pacifying conversations
either we equally share in this nation
or prepare for more violent confrontations

(Jewel #358)
it's all a game to them
political enemies are always friends
no matter which way they bend
the **Globe Holders** play to win
the hands are shaking
the deals are being made
in fact the deals are done
the American people just got played

The Book of Born Free - Volume One

(Jewel #359)
it's time to build new pyramids
wave new scepters
heal new lepers
write new Metu Neters
Sankofa is real
go back and fetch it
but if we don't build something right now
our children will never respect it

(Jewel #360)
my faith is FORTIFIED
my GOD NEVER LIES
I RISE, the prince of TIDES
no time to CRY
UNIFY or DIE
and you know all the reasons WHY
AMPLIFY, DEFY, and summon the courage
of GOD from INSIDE

The Book of Born Free - Volume One

*My Loving
Black Erotica
and my
Delicious Desire
for
Living Right Now!*

The Book of Born Free - Volume One

Prince is ALIVE!

The Book of Born Free - Volume One

MY HEARTS TESTIMONY (unedited -1999)
(this isn't about flow, rhyme, meter, schemes, or verse.
this is my heart cut wide open and poured out on this page.)

I can't believe you're here
I'm so afraid to touch you
afraid to embrace you
terrified to kiss you
for it might reveal
my greatest fear
that you're just
an apparition
a luminous phantasm
a thirsty man's mirage
a mushroomed hallucination
a trick sent by a devil
to trap and bind me
to his bidding
by placing before me
an indescribable beauty
an echo of spring
a spiritual transformation
a gentle smile from God herself
this is insanity at its most delicious
are you angelic or pernicious
or should I just calm down
and not make a sound
and just enjoy the unequaled sunrise
let your light touch my eyes
and just be available
to receive and believe
I'm afraid beloved
I'm afraid to trust again

The Book of Born Free - Volume One

*God knows I'm trying
God knows I'm not lying
but honestly
I still can't believe
you're here
standing before me
attempting to reach inside of me
and resuscitate the mummified memory
of a man that barely existed in the first place
please tell me
how did you find me
my location was hidden
from even myself
a treacherous snake
ate all the breadcrumbs
I was using to announce my path
leaving me to wander bitterly
and aimlessly through
the petrified forests
of my mutilated and abandoned trust
you see I was a few feeble steps away
from accepting this non-life
this broken hope
this shadowy existence
as a full life
a wonderful life
and the only life that I could ever achieve
when you inexplicably appeared
from the dust of a forgotten dream
scattered inside a stale breeze
longing to be forgotten again
and I almost didn't recognize you*

The Book of Born Free - Volume One

but your heavenly aroma
spiritual kiss
deep thoughts
even deeper abyss
Goddess stance
galactic dance
put me back
into a Tantric trance
your righteous shape
believable fate
saved me from
the tongue of the snake
your creamy womb
earthly perfume
saved me from
certain doom
your sugary tears
exotic atmosphere
allowed me to
let go of all my fears
praise be to God
praise be to God
praise be to God
praise be to God
you stimulated my deadened nerves
reconnected my spine to my mind
and my trust to my heart
that allowed me to push time aside
and remember what is was like
to love

Born Free #therealbornfree

The Book of Born Free - Volume One

(Jewel #361)
men and women
were twins from the start
wicked propaganda
drove us apart
search deep inside your heart
and the recesses of your mind
and you'll see our origin
was unified and divine

(Jewel #362)
making love is a beautiful ritual
its creed is sacred and pure
making love should take you to places
you've never been before
every fantasy should be real
every dream should come true
but you must have integrity
in everything you do

(Jewel #363)
our home is our church
our private sanctuary
the place where we were married
and the genesis of our family
our bed is our garden
whose spring harvest will soon yield
God's everlasting spirit
that will bloom in every room

The Book of Born Free - Volume One

(Jewel #364)
I love sitting with you
reciting our songs
writing our Psalms
inside the valley of our palms
drinking our homemade wine
from our golden grail
and celebrating a love
that no one can derail

(Jewel #365)
making love isn't about speed
there's no need to rush
new memories should be created
after every single touch
gradually build your momentum
enjoy every sensation
a lifetime of pleasure can occur
before penetration

The Book of Born Free - Volume One

(Jewel #366)
if these walls could talk
they would speak of a beauty seldom seen
they would talk about a world
most only see in their dreams
they would guide you to the spot
where angels come to sing
and speak about a love
that only God could bring

(Jewel #367)
inside our embrace
we'll unlock ancient mysteries
travel beyond this world
and explore new galaxies
nothing can stop us
no mountain is too high to climb
and we'll burn our disguises
outside the door of God's holiest shrine

(Jewel #368)
you don't need to lose any more weight
you don't need another face
you don't need another nose
you don't need to shorten your toes
you don't need liposuction
or a chemical peel
don't let these unreal images
control how you feel

The Book of Born Free - Volume One

(Jewel #369)
your spiritual activation
moves me towards a monumental ejaculation
your metaphysical meditations
has me caught up in your gravitation
I'm spinning and spiraling
turning and twisting
my hands are behind my back
I'm no longer resisting

(Jewel #370)
if you want to experience love
you must live inside the light
you can't be afraid to say
and do what's right
because love's true power
comes from courage and faith
you'll never feel its embrace
if you continue to play it safe

The Book of Born Free - Volume One

(Jewel #371)
I can't deny your tongue
when it calls I cum
I can't deny your prophecy
you are the one
I can't deny my heart
you are my truth
I can't deny my love for you
I don't need any more proof

(Jewel #372)
our bodies are crashing
our new memories are laughing
our hearts are learning
our flesh is burning
our fingers are romancing
our genitals are dancing
our mouths are asking
our moons are waxing

(Jewel #373)
if you don't have any fetishes
you're not having any fun
accepting your fetish
is like swallowing the sun
it's letting all that liquid heat
pour right through your pores
our fetishes allow us to see
and explore so much more

The Book of Born Free - Volume One

(Jewel #374)
you've cut through my melancholy
you've evaporated my rain
you've given purpose to my folly
you've medicated my pain
you've realigned my stars
you've stopped me from growing old
you've melted my bars
you've given me heaven to hold

(Jewel #375)
mount me
merge with me
open my mouth
and put all your words in me
pour them down my throat
watch my eyes illuminate
this is how Gods
and Goddesses communicate

The Book of Born Free - Volume One

(Jewel #376)
I got in this boat with you
because I trust you
you can put your hands around my throat
because I trust you
you can claim my heart as your sole possession
because I trust you
I willingly submit to all your salacious obsessions
because I trust you

(Jewel #377)
we have more than just sex
and that's why our sex is so fucking good
that's what those love haters
have never understood
they counted us out
but we lasted longer
they loved and lost
but we just keep getting stronger

(Jewel #378)
the rich melanin
inside your skin
vibrates deep within
the mysterious womb of your violin
I thought I knew its source
but it's beyond my measure
licking across your ancient hue
melts away my worldly pressures

The Book of Born Free - Volume One

(Jewel #379)
I feel like a virgin again
everything is terrifying and electrifying
you're filled with chocolate cream
with strawberries inside the lining
I feel so vulnerable
so fresh, so new
and I know this rebirth
is all because of you

(Jewel #380)
what have you done to me
I can feel my blood and brain burn
I have an overwhelming desire to
love, listen, and learn
my heart is alive again
it's bursting right through my chest
you've consumed all of me
and I'm dying a happy death

The Book of Born Free - Volume One

(Jewel #381)
your last text was ablaze
with erotic anticipation
I submit to your declaration
I will forgo all masturbation
my hands and body will be pure
when you enter my door
my soul trembles
every time I hear your eyes roar

(Jewel #382)
we can't be bound
and caged in by tradition
our religion can't be reduced
by shallow definition
our dreams soar beyond
the gates of heaven
we have no time for foolish mortal rumors
and petty internet questions

(Jewel #383)
we will kill anything that attempts
to block our love from the sun
we will spill its blood
and delight as it falls and runs
we will destroy you if you
try to corrupt us with your lies
we will open the gates of hell
if you try to block our love's immortal rise

The Book of Born Free - Volume One

(Jewel #384)
our love has so many
deliciously dangerous layers
it can't be found
in our Lord's most sacred prayers
this is something new
something outside the sky of comprehension
when we make love
we open the gateway to a million new dimensions

(Jewel #385)
you're a living symphony
of thoughts, words, and deeds
lusts and needs
you're a rare flower amongst winter weeds
cut me wide open
and allow me to bleed
all over your sweet garden
and feed our future seeds

The Book of Born Free - Volume One

(Jewel #386)
I welcome you back
with warm outstretched limbs
my love for you erupts
and spills mightily over the brim
I've been asleep in the grave
since we foolishly parted ways
the golden love that we appraised
can't be outweighed or led astray

(Jewel #387)
you've awakened me
I see myself outside of ordinary expectations
outside of mindless congregations
and raging temptations
I don't know what I can accomplish
but I'm ready to face the darkness
burn every harness
and fly regardless

(Jewel #388)
I can feel myself
crumbling into ashes
the fire that flashes
has consumed my casket
all that has been published before
died in all the senseless wars
everything that I once abhorred
I now unabashedly adore

The Book of Born Free - Volume One

(Jewel #389)
come into my house
of outlandish torture
where hot black leather
grows alongside a soft white orchard
penetration of your body
isn't my only destination
I'm probing your depths
to find your soul's secret location

(Jewel #390)
hold me tighter
use your tongue, use your teeth
don't be shy
you can reach underneath
apply more pressure
I might bruise, but I won't break
go deeper and deeper
I want to feel this bed and house violently shake

The Book of Born Free - Volume One

(Jewel #391)
even though we've never made love
our love is deep and abound
we're the only reason
desolation no longer comes around
we were with God as He poured himself
into the first primordial pond
our chemical bond
keeps our souls warm and embalmed

(Jewel #392)
ascend with me
leave all those petty concerns behind
give up trying to change
their ignorant minds
if they can't see that real love
transcends all of this
in the end
their existence won't be remembered or missed

(Jewel #393)
you've penetrated me
you've pushed deep inside my cavity
you've gone passed the boundaries
of my anatomy
the unhappy laughs at me
and calls our love a blasphemy
but they wish they could see your majesty
and experience our divine rhapsody

The Book of Born Free - Volume One

(Jewel #394)
nothing on this earth
can diminish our light
I can feel the intensity of our love
when we argue and fight
no relationship is free from disagreements
or divergent points of view
just know that no matter what's said or done
I'll never stop loving you

(Jewel #395)
your body looks amazing
you look stunning in your clothes
but let's take this beneath the surface
I need to know what you know
what type of person are you
what type of causes do you support
I want to see the last 5 books you bought
and your six-pack thoughts

The Book of Born Free - Volume One

(Jewel #396)
I love thick women with love handles
and chocolate muffin tops
beautifully full breasts
and a devotion that won't stop
sexy round hips with soft feet
that wrinkle perfectly on the bottom
all night private dancer
with wet lips soft as cotton

(Jewel #397)
my feminism looks like me standing
with my Queen on the front lines
shoulder-to-shoulder, heart-to-heart
and mind-to-mind
we can't be torn asunder
what happens to her happens to me
her issues are my issues
and that's the way God intended us to be

(Jewel #398)
what they've shown us of love
is of a rancid complexion
a ghoulish deception
a dying legend
a jaundiced eye
a slow poisonous lie
true love would never want us
to kneel and comply

The Book of Born Free - Volume One

(Jewel #399)
everything that's kinky
doesn't involve restraints
the things we do
make sinners and saints faint
they never knew how succulent
and deep this rabbit hole goes
once the soul is truly exposed
you can cum in and out of clothes

(Jewel #400)
I pull hair
and probe deep with my tongue
don't get in the bed with me
if you're still thinking young
no spot is off limits
this only works if we're committed
don't get in the bed with me
if you're still scared and timid

The Book of Born Free - Volume One

<u>Divinely Ordained - 2000</u>
(a love song waiting 2 be sung)

baby we made it to paradise
we passed the final test
I knew from day one
our life together was blessed
I can feel our love
through every part of our life
and through our heart and soul
we'll walk in heaven tonight
and

to feel this sweet pleasure
we had to go through some pain
but I knew our love was true
it's divinely ordained
many people were called
but only we remain
I knew our love was true
it's divinely ordained

I knew your love was coming
before God sent you
so, giving you my everything
is what I was ***BORN*** *to do*
I love the way you feel
from your lips to your spirit
our love has no limit
our love is fearless

The Book of Born Free - Volume One

and if it takes my last breath
I'll show you how to defeat death
cuz if love is a battlefield
we'll be the last soldiers left
And

to feel this sweet pleasure
we had to go through some pain
but I knew our love was true
it's divinely ordained
many people were called
but only we remain
I knew our love was true
it's divinely ordained

and we were married from day one
beloved, moon and sun
with an eternity of ecstasy
flowing when we cum
and if it takes my last breath
I'll show you how to defeat death
cuz if love is a battlefield
we'll be the last soldiers left
And

to feel this sweet pleasure
we had to go through some pain
but I knew our love was true
it's divinely ordained
many people were called
but only we remain
I knew our love was true
it's divinely ordained

Born Free #therealbornfree

The Book of Born Free - Volume One

(Jewel #401)
everything around you
shows the bitter signs of times harsh evidence
your beauty stands defiant
and gives us an unchanging relevance
even the air ages
and gets denser and thicker
but your sweet artistry
just keeps getting younger and quicker

(Jewel #402)
how can I live away from you
your exquisiteness spoiled me to ruin
if our confluence is separated
my sanity will be loosened
I don't care if begging you to stay
makes me a pitiful human
this is a consecrated union
the truth behind the illusion

(Jewel #403)
our love is sacrosanct
and the most hallowed ground
these words that I expound
are for more than just sound
we've built a new Eden
of wondrous enchantment
that will ruthlessly annihilate
hate's growing encampment

The Book of Born Free - Volume One

(Jewel #404)
tub full of roses
candles all around
radiator on high
making that whistle sound
the moon is shining through
the stained-glass sky light
take a big bite
we might fuck around and make a baby tonight

(Jewel #405)
read me something nasty
feed me from your unpublished book
pass me those bright red ribbons
and those stainless-steel hooks
I'll get the grapefruit
you get the cranberry vodka and ice
this is the good life
let's pray and give our last rites

The Book of Born Free - Volume One

(Jewel #406)
you are my poetry
every letter, and every word
you are my every idea
every verse, and every inclination stirred
you are my every quote
every sonnet, and every lascivious phrase
you are a part of everything
that I've ever spilled out on the page

(Jewel #407)
the morning has arrived
Frankie Beverly serenades
we fall to our knees
and give thanks for the new day God made
last night isn't over
this is just a momentary cessation
our wanton exploration
will end in drenched jubilation

(Jewel #408)
I love that we can talk
for hours upon hours
each link that we construct
weakens their power
we kiss with righteous insolence
and drown out their jeers
we smashed their veneer
now everything they created disappears

The Book of Born Free - Volume One

(Jewel #409)
I love your sticky fingers
which hand do you use when I'm not home
how far do you go
to make yourself quiver and moan
do you play with your nipples
do you call out my name
how deep do you have to go
to make your pussy squirt and rain

(Jewel #410)
before you approach her
ask yourself if you truly deserve her
because without sincerity and integrity
you'll never keep her
if you want that magic to occur
met her on the highest levels
it takes more than chocolate rose petals
to find where Heaven is settled

The Book of Born Free - Volume One

(Jewel #411)
our love is only possible
by our God's evolving plan
ignorance and laziness
causes some misunderstand
they mock our joy
with their thoughts and their hands
but we'll be redeemed
by our God's demand

(Jewel #412)
I've fallen so deeply in love
that I've buried myself alive
being completely open
is the only way I'll survive
hope runs rampant
beneath our celestial bedspread
and sheds God's eternal light
on our bright future ahead

(Jewel #413)
every time I taste your flesh
it feels like the first time
we have no beginning or ending
when our bodies our entwined
ecstasy is calling
let us not decline
the heavens have sent us their blessing
inside the stars aligned

The Book of Born Free - Volume One

(Jewel #414)
come bathe with me
let's baptize ourselves in God's favorite stream
let's wash away the darkness
that tries to come in between
let's pour fresh water
on our souls to revive our bond
let's submerge in the everlasting
and fly beyond

(Jewel #415)
don't be afraid
of our mystical orgasm
don't run away from
our erotic soul spasm
these blessings are the fruits
of our love's labor
the intimate way of our savior
is to eat slow and savor

The Book of Born Free - Volume One

(Jewel #416)
feast on me
make a meal of my curiosities and hopes
look at me unflinchingly
and declare that we're forever yoked
use our love to strengthen your convictions
and fortify your spirit
grab my hand with the force of God
and never, ever release it

(Jewel #417)
beautiful is too common a phrase
to place by your gentle feet
your eyes have made
the sun and moon obsolete
when God placed you on my shores
he knew revolution would follow
and our love would drive despair
back into the shadows

(Jewel #418)
our neighbors know
these walls are too thin
they heard us making love
over and over and over again
they heard the pots and pans clanging
they felt the headboard banging
they heard you swallowing
after I gave you a serious spanking

The Book of Born Free - Volume One

(Jewel #419)
I love kissing you
right after I cum in your mouth
I don't care about the amount
the feeling is paramount
while others shy away
we gorge ourselves without delay
no matter what they portray
they're not ready for this level of play

(Jewel #420)
did you masturbate like I instructed
did you complete the task
did you lubricate with coconut oil
before you invaded your ass
did you watch the video
of us fucking in the summer rain
when did you realize
that your life would never be the same

The Book of Born Free - Volume One

(Jewel #421)
my love for you doesn't oppress me
it liberates me
it envelops me
it allows me to be exactly what I need to be
it gives me the confidence
to confront oppression and depression
it showed me how to let go of my pain
and start counting my blessings

(Jewel #422)
tonight my mind is drifting
and slipping into the abyss
lost in our dream where pain
and pleasure lovingly exist
we're twin flames
engaged in risqué role play
in a universe where night is day
and the greatest desire is to obey

(Jewel #423)
it's hard to put into words
just what you've done for me
you've tamed my tempest
and pruned the dead leaves on my tree
our bedroom is on fire
with the intensity of our passion's heat
and the fact that we're in love
makes this moment blissfully sweet

The Book of Born Free - Volume One

(Jewel #424)
I've been lost in the petrified forests
of my mutilated trust
until you showed me the bridge
between my true love and my pure lust
I'm completely intoxicated
by your natural angelic musk
I'm so full of joy, love, and laughter
that I just might bust

(Jewel #425)
this is insanity
in its rawest form
this is us
before we were born
before we were torn
and left for dead
our souls contain a scripture
that has never been read

The Book of Born Free - Volume One

(Jewel #426)
love is patient
it waits for us at eternity's altar
love is strength
it does not falter
but as we drag our feet
we reveal a soul incomplete
she will not grab our hands
if we won't let go of the devil's feet

(Jewel #427)
love prays for us
its song calls us to the stage
love is purity
it smells like fresh sage
but as we misinterpret
and mangle its intention
our names will cease
to be spoken in her dimension

(Jewel #428)
love is perceptive
it sees our deception with a trillion eyes
love forgives
it doesn't condemn us for our lies
but if we continue
to plot and scheme
she will hide her true face
from our visions and dreams

The Book of Born Free - Volume One

(Jewel #429)
love is walking on air
it has no weight
love is indestructible
it will never break
but she will not carry our bags
or bear our petty burdens
she will close her ears
to our selfish pleas and sermons

(Jewel #430)
love is unpredictable
it plays without thought or care
love is constant
it will always be there
but she will not share
with ungrateful beings
she's very leery of those
who are double dealing

The Book of Born Free - Volume One

(Jewel #431)
love is vigilant
it's forever on watch
love is timeless
it knows no clock
but she frowns on those
who waste precious moments
and she will drop you from the sky
without any notice

(Jewel #432)
love is studious
it's constantly learning
love is wisdom
its bridges are never burning
but she will not sit with us
if we choose to remain in the dark
she will not open the door
after God closes the ark

(Jewel #433)
love is grounded
it's one of us
love speaks our language
it has a reservoir to discuss
but she won't tell us her secrets
if we're unworthy
and afraid to step out
on her father's divine journey

The Book of Born Free - Volume One

(Jewel #434)
love is all seeing
it sits on the highest perch
love is a fortune teller
it's the holy church
but she won't let you
lead her astray
she won't let you block her view
of heaven's creamy Milky Way

(Jewel #435)
love is God
it's everywhere at all times
love is abundance
it connects our hearts and minds
but she won't show us
the path to infinity
if we abandon our children
in this cold world of uncertainty

The Book of Born Free - Volume One

(Jewel #436)
suffocate me with your love
drown me in your desire
cut me with your touch
burn me with your fire
poison me with your lust
kidnap me with your wish
strangle me with your hope
murder me with your kiss

(Jewel #437)
you don't have to be cautious
let your animal out of her cage
I'm dying to see the thin line
between passion and rage
you have my permission to attack me
come rip me to shreds
just as long as you bury me
under the pillow on your side of the bed

(Jewel #438)
all lovers
have been lovers before
true love can't be stopped
or given any permanent detours
love and lovers can't be separated
by death, space, or time
they'll always be together in different
flesh, flowers, and wind chimes

The Book of Born Free - Volume One

(Jewel #439)
if you can't #sayhername
keep mine out of your fucking' mouth
loving and honoring black women
is what I'm all about
black man, our petty beefs
have played right into the devil's plans
we've allowed him to snatch God's greatest gift
right out of our hands

(Jewel #440)
brothers don't support or perpetuate
America's rape culture
it's devilish and vulgar
it's a cancerous ulcer
protect and serve the women in your life
put it all on the line
she's divine and the real reason
God has allowed you to shine

The Book of Born Free - Volume One

<u>Strings - 2000</u>
(a love song waiting 2 be sung)

we need to slow down
baby, what's comes next
what we're about to do
is more than sex
I'm cool with your man
you're best friends with my wife
this shit right here
will affect the rest of our life
cuz there's

no such thing as no strings
someone's bound to get hurt
it might feel good at the start
but in the end it never works
these feelings will pass
this ain't gonna last
we'll lose everything
cuz there's no such thing as no strings

I'm not saying I don't want you
I can barely hold myself back
but what's gonna happen
after we do that
baby I'm about to slip
don't tempt me with those hips
cuz I'm about to betray
every word coming from my lips

and what's gonna happen
when we link up as friends
will we be able to play it cool
or will jealously come in
cuz there's

The Book of Born Free - Volume One

no such thing as no strings
someone's bound to get hurt
it might feel good at the start
but in the end it never works
these feelings will pass
this ain't gonna last
we'll lose everything
cuz there's no such thing as no strings

baby I do want you
but we should stop before we start
I don't want to be responsible
for breaking 4 hearts
we've already crossed the line
we must be out of our damn minds
we can't go back
and rewind time

and what's gonna happen
when we link up as friends
will we be able to play it cool
or will jealously come in
cuz there's

no such thing as no strings
someone's bound to get hurt
it might feel good at the start
but in the end it never works
these feelings will pass
this ain't gonna last
we'll lose everything
cuz there's no such thing as no strings

Born Free #therealbornfree

The Book of Born Free - Volume One

(Jewel #441)
I don't care about how or why
I accept your heart without hesitation
our world is open and free
we don't need reservations
our love is an affirmation
a holy confirmation
and every time we make love
we give birth to something new in creation

(Jewel #442)
I love when you lay back
and slowly play with your clit
I love when you massage your breasts
as I kiss your inner thighs and hips
I hope you brought the red wine
and those black cherry-scented candle sticks
all hell is going to break loose
when I open my new chocolate tool kit

(Jewel #443)
beloved really look at me
I know my heart carries a lot of ugly scars
please don't be afraid
to read the pages of my memoir
I know you'll be able to relate
and feel what I narrate
it's a beautiful passion play
about loves great victory over betrayal and hate

The Book of Born Free - Volume One

(Jewel #444)
we've created our own language
inside our own little cult
some try to insult
because they're afraid of open-minded adults
we love who we want
we fuck who we want
and while they gawk and front
we're living the life that they secretly want

(Jewel #445)
most days I don't need to be fucked
I just need to be kissed
given a spiritual lift
and acknowledged that I exist
I need to know that I'm worth the risk
and that I'll be missed
it's simple things like this
that bring me the deepest feelings of bliss

The Book of Born Free - Volume One

(Jewel #446)
your beauty has winter in submission
you've broken all its icy teeth
you've released all the souls frozen
and tormented by grief
even in the shadow of your gaze
you illuminate sun rays
the warmth of your love
protects me from winter's brutal decay

(Jewel #447)
don't ever leave me
stand where I stand
if we squander this love
our souls will be forever damned
if we fail to take advantage
of all this ecstasy, happiness, and truth
God will be forced
to close our eyes and cut us loose

(Jewel #448)
they call us wild savages
because our love is loud and suspicious
it's sinfully sweet
and carnally capricious
it's born of the stars
but rooted in earth
it's a mixture of a hedonistic penetration
and an immaculate birth

The Book of Born Free - Volume One

(Jewel #449)
I used to look upon the future
with dread and uneasy residence
my movements were slow
and full of childish hesitance
but with you in my life
my chest swells, and my legs stand unyielding
you taught me that love
is the only sword worth wielding

(Jewel #450)
when Trump won
I started to rage and despair
you quickly blew love in the air
and led our temple in prayer
when we opened our eyes
you told us to rise
you put a gun and the Torah in my hands
and said, "God Provides!"

The Book of Born Free - Volume One

(Jewel #451)
neither one of us were virgins
when we first met
we tasted the sweetness of victory
and spat out the bitterness of regret
beloved our friendship and love
was preordained and overdue
our walls cracked just enough
for God's healing light to shine through

(Jewel #452)
our enemies gathered overhead
cold venom drips from their fangs
jealously explodes in their bellies
with violent ricochets and pangs
these vultures fly in circles over our bed
waiting for our love to die
but our love shoots laser beams
and blasts them out of the sky

(Jewel #453)
I feel the wine is turning me up
and your soft hands are laying me down
just like I felt your heart pound
beneath your white wedding gown
we're the last two people on earth
who truly see and believe
and that's why God has blessed us
to be the next Adam and Eve

The Book of Born Free - Volume One

(Jewel #454)
I love colorful ink
on beautiful black skin
these new prolific hieroglyphics
reveal the truth hidden within
these signs and symbols
give me a glimpse of your buried treasure
I could spend the rest of my life
reading from your fleshy ledger

(Jewel #455)
my Queen flows from home pole stripping
to field strippin'
cookin', knittin'
and back to RBG set trippin'
she's into head splittin' and godly transmittin'
there's no open admission
you must ask permission before steppin' into her kitchen

The Book of Born Free - Volume One

(Jewel #456)
our love is the seed, the water
the sun, and the vine
our love is the hand, the glass
the lips, and the wine
our love is the thought, the word
the moment, and the action
our love is the touch, the stimulation
the execution, and the satisfaction

(Jewel #457)
I love when you resist a little
and make me work hard for my dinner
you've made it **Crystal** clear
you don't have time for beginners
so I pulled back the sheets
and showed you my expertise
watched you lovingly submit
and now everything is peace

(Jewel #458)
I can't stop writing
I'm compelled to record our story
I need to leave a book
for all the men that follow me
they need to know that true love
is reachable and tangible
they need to know that love is completely graspable
and absolutely magical

The Book of Born Free - Volume One

(Jewel #459)
I don't spank you because I hate you
I spank you because I love you
adore you, revere you
and would do anything for you
this is our world
I will allow your lover to cum in
but they must be honest with themselves
before we begin

(Jewel #460)
your love has me spinning
like an ecstatic dervish
at first, I was nervous
but now I'm completely at your service
our love can be loosely described
but it can't be pronounced
all doubts and distractions
must be rejected and denounced

The Book of Born Free - Volume One

(Jewel #461)
if you just want to hit and run
don't use love's name
if you just want some meaningless fun
don't use love's name
if you just want a hot body on a cold night
don't use love's name
if you won't be around to see the morning light
don't use love's name

(Jewel #462)
before you move forward
ask yourself some serious questions
are you ready for free
and open expression
are you ready to put your life
in your lover's hands
are you ready to live and die right
where your lover stands

(Jewel #463)
are you ready to live with
their strengths and weaknesses
are you ready to accept
their sour and sweetness's
are you ready to help them
build and maintain their occupation
are you ready to have
a non-judgmental conversation

The Book of Born Free - Volume One

(Jewel #464)
are you ready to put your lover's needs
ahead of yours
are you ready to help them fight and win
a righteous war
are you ready to love them
in word and deed
are you ready to give them
the keys to succeed

(Jewel #465)
are you ready to share
their spiritual vision
are you ready to walk with them
on a spiritual mission
are you ready to give them
a spiritual ministration
are you ready to help them
build a home on a spiritual foundation

The Book of Born Free - Volume One

(Jewel #466)
I love holding your ankles
and pushing your feet towards the headboard
I love when you scream in wild ecstasy
to be rescued by our Lord
every time I go deeper
I can feel the heat of a million suns
you're the only one
who has ever truly made me cum

(Jewel #467)
you look enticing this morning
don't take another step
with each breath
we dive to a deeper depth
your thighs are soaking wet
my organ is engorged
we're going to leave the outline of Heaven
on your bedroom floor

(Jewel #468)
before Instagram, Snapchat, and Twitter
we were in love
before Tumblr, Vine, and YouTube
we were in love
before Facebook, Myspace, and Blackplanet
we were in love
before our parent's parents were born
we were in love

The Book of Born Free - Volume One

(Jewel #469)
love, music
and organic food
chocolate, candles
and a sexy mood
imagination, creativity
and flexibility
leads to elevation, divinity
and infinite possibilities

(Jewel #470)
when you came over
we had no idea what was about to transpire
but we've always known
that we contained this raging fire
it started as soon as you came in
and went until you walked out the door
I'm still having flashbacks
of you on all fours on the kitchen floor

The Book of Born Free - Volume One

(Jewel #471)
my wounds were fatal
my death was certain
I made peace with my passing
I bowed before the final curtain
I was ready to let the bitter chill of December
wash over my skin
but your love wouldn't let me go
your love wouldn't let me give in

(Jewel #472)
with all the death and violence
surrounding our home
death by police, death by phone
and death by drone
you insolate us
you shield us with all the happiness that you contain
you take away the pain
and keep us unstained by the mark of Cain

(Jewel #473)
when you showed me your extensive bookshelf
I KNEW!
when you taught me how to strengthen my health
I KNEW!
when you turned off the TV to meditate without a sound
I KNEW!
when you told me your desire to burn Babylon down
I KNEW!

The Book of Born Free - Volume One

(Jewel #474)
your virtue
isn't wrapped up in virginity
your tattoos
haven't marred your ingenuity
I don't judge you
by your tongue's vulgarity
for me, you're the perfect blend
of dark fantasy and a stark reality

(Jewel #475)
I love when we
train together
I love when we get through
the pain together
our bodies must be
as strong as our spirits
because my dearest
the war will be at our door within minutes

The Book of Born Free - Volume One

(Jewel #476)
nothing before you
prepared me for this
I am embarrassed that I approached you
so unequipped
for so long I was in love
with my own immature ego and laughter
but when I read through your first few chapters
I knew I wanted to die next to you where the angels gather

(Jewel #477)
I've searched
the caverns of reason
seen stronger men and women
falter and weaken
they falsely believed
that true love was unreachable
so God released them from the class
and graded them un-teachable

(Jewel #478)
this is the real thing
the marriage before the ring
the deep joy you felt the first time
you heard Aretha sing
the first day of spring
the great fortune that comes from a dove's wing
the simple sound of love
that overwhelms the ordinary Hotline Bling

The Book of Born Free - Volume One

(Jewel #479)
we were married
before the ceremony
no acrimony
our whole story is a holy matrimony
we defy all categories
our love is a beautiful allegory
we flourish in uncharted territories
because we give God all the glory

(Jewel #480)
before you get too close
and those passionate fires get stoked
please take note
to see if you're equally yoked
go deeper than common movies
and favorite recipes
do you see the same spiritually
and can you mutually raise a family

The Book of Born Free - Volume One

(Jewel #481)
I've been overly cautious
I've been inching and inching along
but it's not because
you did anything wrong
I'm a bag lady
I'm carrying around a lot of unclaimed freight
and I didn't want you to get crushed
under an avalanche of my dead weight

(Jewel #482)
most kick God out of the bedroom
but we give him a front row seat
without his permission
our orgasms would be incomplete
love is our religion
trust is our religion
God and sex are only separated
by our bad decisions

(Jewel #483)
I love that your blackness
goes beyond your hue
I love that you make the men in your life
rise higher than you
I love that you're a crafty leader
and a strong backbone
I love that you can turn any empty space
into a loving African home

The Book of Born Free - Volume One

(Jewel #484)
we live by Mosaic Laws
and recite Langston Hughes prayers
the scriptures of Sonia Sanchez
guide us up the stairs
the songs of Shalom
set in motion our hands and feet
and the glory of Yahweh
blesses all the food we eat

(Jewel #485)
it's our mutual love of God
that makes our love unbeatable
it's our full commitment to YAH
that makes our love unbreakable
it's our total trust in each other
that makes our love undeniable
it's our universal faith in humanity
that makes our love unstoppable

The Book of Born Free - Volume One

(Jewel #486)
naysayers come and go
like the ebb and flow of ocean tides
it's fun to watch their hatred
slowly drown and die
as they gasp for air
and the saltwater fills their blackened lungs
we're having fun on the beach
making love under the golden sun

(Jewel #487)
we kiss in Swahili
we're filled with the passion of the Fulani
our Habari Gani
is filled with joyous Imani
African love making
is the original love making
the nectar from your Nile Valley
is creamy and amazing

(Jewel #488)
I don't want you sedated
I don't want you degraded
I don't want you inebriated
I don't want you incapacitated
I need your eyes wide open
I need your mind unbroken
I need you outspoken
I need you full of love and emotion

The Book of Born Free - Volume One

(Jewel #489)
separation doesn't always separate
break down, and disintegrate
wipe away or plunder
curse or tear asunder
sometimes we need
to be shocked back to reality
shown calamity
and reintroduced to gravity

(Jewel #490)
if I tell the world that I worship you
they'll call me a blasphemer
if I say that you're my redeemer
they'll say I'm a non-believer
if I tell the world that you're my healer
they'll say I'm sick with fever
but since God made me a love seeker
I willingly submit to my new teacher

The Book of Born Free - Volume One

(Jewel #491)
I love being a part of us
I love being accountable
commitment has given us
a love more fruitful and bountiful
some say we're corny
some say we're so plain jane
but we just continue in our slow lane
flying above all the thunderous rain

(Jewel #492)
I can't wait until we get home
pull over right here
don't worry about the police
let go of your fear
I love when you beg
and you love when I plead
baby follow me to the backseat
and just follow my lead

(Jewel #493)
I love your mouth
it holds the answers to my most ambitious wish
I've waited my entire life
to taste a delicious kiss like this
the magnitude of the moment
brings me down to my knees
I love when your jaws squeeze
and milk my cum and soul out with ease

The Book of Born Free - Volume One

(Jewel #494)
I've tried to find the right words
to convey my hearts truest mind
unbind myself from the falsehoods
that marked my immature times
I've resigned my purpose
to giving you the ripest fruits from my vine
God grant me mercy
on this hallowed mountain I climb

(Jewel #495)
your body is my territory
I'm in total command
when you leave here today
you'll know you've been touched by a man
everything is moving
according to my pornographic plan
from this day forward
your flesh, heart, and spirit will carry my brand

The Book of Born Free - Volume One

Sweetwater Farms - 2001
(a love song waiting 2 be sung)

I got an email the other day
for a free getaway
I'm so ready
to get out and play
I invited my girl euphoria
she's a lot of fun
and I secretly wanted
her to be the one
as soon as we got there
the music blared
we both could feel
the magic in the air

and down at Sweetwater Farms
the beds float on blueberry clouds
the maids wore French braids
under silky white shrouds
they sing African Lullaby's
baked sweet potato pies
down at Sweetwater Farms
no soul has ever died

we took the whirlwind tour
saw things we've never seen before
unicorns in cars
8-foot Minotaur's
a blind woman
blew bubbles from liquid stars
children played with their dreams
on Hendricks old guitar

at first it was crazy
but now we live without a care

The Book of Born Free - Volume One

cuz we both could feel
the magic in the air

and down at Sweetwater Farms
the beds float on blueberry clouds
the maids wore French braids
under silky white shrouds
they sing African Lullaby's
baked sweet potato pies
down at Sweetwater Farms
no soul has ever died

it was a perfect balance
between sunshine and rain
we forgot about fear
we forgot about pain
it was beyond all words
it was what it was
and then we looked at each other
and confessed our eternal love

at first it was crazy
but now we live without a care
cuz we both could feel
the magic in the air

and down at Sweetwater Farms
the beds float on blueberry clouds
the maids wore French braids
under silky white shrouds
they sing African Lullaby's
baked sweet potato pies
down at Sweetwater Farms
no soul has ever died

Born Free #therealbornfree

The Book of Born Free - Volume One

(Jewel #496)
Nefertiti is jealous
of your otherworldly beauty
Isis can't match
the righteousness of your duty
Ma'at worships
your grace and balance
Makeda knows
she can't match your womanly challenge

(Jewel #497)
next to you
the rest pale in comparison
imposters are arrested
by Gods holy garrison
miracles follow your footsteps
as you travel through the hemisphere
those who try to impersonate
your angelic stare will wilt and disappear

(Jewel #498)
we've traveled light years
into the future and we're greater than before
the stars that used to shine above
now decorate our bedroom floor
we've broken free from our binds
we make love outside of time
the world inside our home
reflects God's eternal and loving mind

The Book of Born Free - Volume One

(Jewel #499)
I never knew that madness
would make me feel so happy
I never thought that that finding love
would make my friends so angry
I never knew that my body
could bend in so many different positions
I never thought I would find
someone with the same sensual volition

(Jewel #500)
sex feels better when there's love
tastes sweeter with friendship
sex feels better when there's dialogue
tastes sweeter with commitment
sex feels better when there's trust
tastes sweeter with intellect
sex feels better when there's imagination
tastes sweeter with respect

The Book of Born Free - Volume One

(Jewel #501)
can you hear the flames roar
and the embers crackle
this kind of sex was made
for a supernatural tabernacle
I don't believe in taboos
I believe in me and you
sip this erotic brew
and let's ravage each other in the back of the pew

(Jewel #502)
I haven't slept
since the day we met
I also haven't had
a single moment of regret
I haven't lied, cried
or been sarcastic
I've been fantastic, cinematic
and full of extreme black magic

(Jewel #503)
you've always been intelligently explosive
and erotically precocious
untamed, unclaimed
and wildly ferocious
at first, I was afraid
for my mortal life
but once I saw your wings in the light
I knew you were my wife

The Book of Born Free - Volume One

(Jewel #504)
the middle of our bed
has become our most sacred ground
you're my Queen
and tonight, you will be crowned
our dream catchers along the wall
will record our nightly activities
our black angels will be witnesses
to our most libidinous proclivities

(Jewel #505)
I lose all control
whenever you come in my vicinity
your decadent divinity
is wrapped inside raw obscenity
I'm nothing but clay
upon your potter's wheel
you have the power to create and break me
whenever you feel

The Book of Born Free - Volume One

(Jewel #506)
venetian masks
non-stop orgies
it's true that sex is better
after forty
no games
just elevated planes
no mental chains
you can travel freely in and out of all lanes

(Jewel #507)
I'm not hurt
that you slept with your girlfriend
we're all due one or two
lost drunken weekends
and since it happened before me
I'm not threatened by the tale
so as I pour the wine
reveal every single nasty detail

(Jewel #508)
hold that pose
the camera loves you tonight
the next 1,000 pictures
will be in glorious black and white
I love the way your eyes dance
between the darkness and the light
devouring your body
is the only thing that calms my appetite

The Book of Born Free - Volume One

(Jewel #509)
as soon as we walked in
we saw bodies on top of bodies
human furniture
strangers fucking in the lobby
somebody tapped me on the shoulder
somebody caught your eye
tonight is the night
that everything will be tested and tried

(Jewel #510)
I love your natural hair
I love your naked soul
I love your unlimited mind
I love your sweet casserole
I love your revolutionary heart
I love your erotic poetry
I love your spiritual prayers
I love your sacred geometry

The Book of Born Free - Volume One

(Jewel #511)
I'm in agony
I can barely move or speak
my mind is baffled
by your mesmerizing mystique
I've spent my whole life
begging God to send you
only to realize
I never really deserved you

(Jewel #512)
don't be afraid to be
natural and primitive
don't be afraid to go beyond
how this world wants you to live
God has given us everything
that we need and yearn for
we stupidly turned every beautiful sensation
into a silly gender war

(Jewel #513)
are you ready to submit
I have your favorite honey-scented nipple clips
mocha covered studs
and strawberry-flavored whips
I'm your lover, your man
your King, your black grip
and whenever we spin the bottle
our roles switch and flip

The Book of Born Free - Volume One

(Jewel #514)
your perfumed body is entrapment
you lured me into your web
all you had to do
was leave your Jewel Box open on your bed
my fingerprints are all over your body
you have my full confession
locking me up inside your love
is the only way to teach me a lesson

(Jewel #515)
my hands are not worthy
to touch your hem
I would die
if we had to live as platonic friends
when it comes to you
I don't know how to pause
for a single kiss
I would break Heaven's laws

The Book of Born Free - Volume One

(Jewel #516)
being intensely experimental
is romantic to us
fucking hard and fast
is romantic to us
being inappropriate and outrageous
is romantic to us
talking raw and dirty
is romantic to us

(Jewel #517)
I need all my lovers
to be readers
and thrill ride
curiosity seekers
killers of wicked
and greedy leaders
full-time love
and life breeders

(Jewel #518)
we're not finished love
catch your breath
tonight, we're putting all that text talk
to the ultimate test
get back into position
let's push past our limits
I need to be implicit
I want to cum inside your spirit

The Book of Born Free - Volume One

(Jewel #519)
I've never been this emotional
this open, and this ready
this honest, this willing
and this steady
this hopeful, this loving
and this sexy
this thirsty, this hungry
or this clumsy

(Jewel #520)
I love this time of night
when the world is tucked in
our sacred sin
is about to begin
nothing is off the menu
our imagination is ambitious
obscene and twisted
each bite is righteously wicked

The Book of Born Free - Volume One

(Jewel #521)
it's the **Rebirth of the Flesh**
cum take a bite
it's **Xtralovable**
All Day, All Night
my ex **Camille** looked into her **Crystal Ball**
at the **Dream Factory**
and saw **200 Balloons** flying free
the moment I came inside your **Scarlett Pussy**

(Jewel #522)
I know what you're thinking
I can read your **Dirty Mind**
each thought sought
is intimately entwined with mine
When Eye Lay My Hands on U
my **Fury** will leave you **Satisfied**
I'm **The One U Wanna C**
when it gets cold outside

(Jewel #523)
baby this is that **Good Love**
celebrate the **Joy in Repetition**
mastering every position in the **Kamasutra**
is our only mission
Coincidence or Fate?
I believe we were inevitable
that's why each **Kiss** is pleasurable
and forever memorable

The Book of Born Free - Volume One

(Jewel #524)
from atop the **Graffiti Bridge**
we marveled at the **Roadhouse Garden**
Adonis and Bathsheba were on the grass
coloring outside the margins
they're always so playful
with nothing but magical things to say
before we flew away, they said **God is Alive**
It's a Wonderful Day

(Jewel #525)
over **Starfish and Coffee**
we talked about this **Strange Relationship**
our **Electric Intercourse**
feeds the **Power Fantastic**
after we listened to the **Voice Inside**
all doubt was gone
our **Moonbeam Levels** revealed the sign
Welcome 2 the Dawn

The Book of Born Free - Volume One

(Jewel #526)
we haven't touched our wine
but we're both intoxicated
we haven't looked at the time
and not a moment has been wasted
we have a clear view
of what all the stargazers strain to see
the first constellation created by God
that secretly whispers to all of humanity

(Jewel #527)
if you're in the battle of the sexes
you're a fool beyond your years
I won't get caught up in the bullshit
with my lonely peers
don't let your broken heart fester
and turn into a malignant cancer
because ignorant banter and wicked slander
is the devil's answer

(Jewel #528)
allow me to wash your feet
allow me to pour warm oil on your toes
allow me to massage your back
allow me to remove all your clothes
allow me to use my mouth
allow me to use my hands
allow me to fuck you
right where you stand

The Book of Born Free - Volume One

(Jewel #529)
I wanted your flesh
but I had to reach passed it to get it
you set the bar higher than image
and my human limits
I was shocked
I've never had such a powerful challenger
I should've known a woman of your caliber
would wield Excalibur

(Jewel #530)
I married you
the moment I met you
the key that sits in me
opened the door that lives in you
the river that I swim in-in my dreams
goes right past your backyard
the prayers that you say at your table
were taught to me by my God

The Book of Born Free - Volume One

(Jewel #531)
it's time to slow things down
life is moving too fast
take off your shoes
and come lay with me on the grass
I feel so connected to you
and everything in creation
right now our souls
are having the deepest conversation

(Jewel #532)
glass dildos, handcuffs
and Ben WA balls
I'm not greedy
but I want to experience it all
every flavor, every smell
every feeling
I'm tired of walking through life
conceding and concealing

(Jewel #533)
leather, latex
and lingerie
catsuits, cock rings
and cannabis spread out on a silver tray
red lights, black lights
and absolutely no lights
no fights, no worries
and no end in sight

The Book of Born Free - Volume One

(Jewel #534)
we speak in verses of desire
and scriptures of pleasure
the fabric of our lives
is intimately sewn together
weaved by the beautifully
aged hands of Oshun
she dresses us in the way
all perfumed lovers should be groomed

(Jewel #535)
I want more than just a quickie
more than just a peek
more than just a lost weekend
more than just 9 1/2 weeks
more than just a promise
more than just the 64 arts
more than just your parts
I want your whole heart

The Book of Born Free - Volume One

(Jewel #536)
before you pick the person
to grow old with
make sure they're also the person
that you can go broke with
cuz when those no money days come
and we know about those days
you need a partner that will have your back
and not selfishly run away

(Jewel #537)
you can be wrong in front of me
you can reveal all your flaws
you can pull down the walls
you no longer have to withdraw
you can trust me
with without investigation
you can trust my word
without any outside confirmation

(Jewel #538)
stop throwing old lover's
back in new lover's face
establish a no-fly zone
for old demons in today's airspace
learn how to truly forgive
don't keep digging up old graves
your new relationship can't be free
if your heart and mind is still enslaved

The Book of Born Free - Volume One

(Jewel #539)
if you can't forgive
you can't expect to be forgiven
grudges cause division
and leave you broken and imprisoned
I burned away all my old hurt feelings
and stopped the bleeding
but if you can't do the same
our love will eventually stop breathing

(Jewel #540)
I've said goodbye to the **Undertaker**
our love won't die on my watch
it's time to take this inner-course
up another notch
I renounce unnatural death
I rebuke cowardly separations
our conscious copulation
fertilized the future right before her ovulation

The Book of Born Free - Volume One

(Jewel #541)
inside our secret confession
a more abundant love begs to be
as we unlock our locks
we throw away our keys
our souls speak in an ancient tongue
only a few can comprehend
as we continue to melt and blend
our spirits ascend

(Jewel #542)
I was broken into a million pieces
ravens picked away at my bones
my name was unknown
I forgot my way home
when I was at my lowest
and I was completely confused
you showed me your true heart
and my world was renewed

(Jewel #543)
I'm not interested
in being right all the time
I could give a damn
about being at the front of the line
I just want to be with you
this is where I belong
trusting each other
is what makes our love so strong

The Book of Born Free - Volume One

(Jewel #544)
I want to be naïve
I want to believe without thinking
I want to look into the eyes of inevitable pain
without blinking
I want to open the windows
and fall in love with every unknown sound
I want to be here with you
when all the walls come crashing down

(Jewel #545)
I love your natural electricity
your mahogany pornography
your sense and sensibility
your perfect indecency
your majestic nobility
your sexy tendencies
your naughty anatomy
your erotic philosophies

The Book of Born Free - Volume One

(Jewel #546)
enveloped by a garden
baptized in the light
christened by stardust
illuminated throughout the night
Heaven is your birthright
you emerged from the Supreme Being
even if God said I was dreaming
I'd still be blessed beyond all meaning

(Jewel #547)
I was Born Free
but now I desire to be enslaved
this warm being I crave
has me willingly caged inside her cave
I want to feel her wash all over me
like a million tidal waves
all my rights I waive
I will even follow her into the grave

(Jewel #548)
if you sit around with your friends
and run down your mate
what do you think
will be your fate
if you sit around with your friends
and elevate your mate
what do you think
will be your fate

The Book of Born Free - Volume One

(Jewel #549)
just stop
you're not a THOT
whoever started that shit
needs to be shot!
you can love
and show off your sexual self
without lowering
and disrespecting yourself

(Jewel #550)
being erotic doesn't mean
that I do not have morals or self-respect
it does not mean you can approach me
without your manners in check
it means that I know who I am
and I'm not afraid to be myself
it means my life won't be determined
by the opinions of everybody else

The Book of Born Free - Volume One

(Jewel #551)
we fell in love
at a self-defense class
the way she fondled her weapon
made me take off my mask
her knowledge of God, gun
moon and sun
made me calculate her sum
as the only ONE!

(Jewel #552)
more than ornamental
more than mere incandescent light
you ignite a fury
beyond what the stars around Christ could ever recite
I dare not approach you
with callow childlike steps
you hold the key to the chamber
where my deepest yearnings are kept

(Jewel #553)
let's go to the garden
bring the fresh fruit and white wine
we need to map out
our next 10,000 lifetimes
let's work out where we're going
to reconnect and re-emerge
let's set our clocks for the next time
all the planets converge

The Book of Born Free - Volume One

(Jewel #554)
incredibly scrumptious
magically wondrous
spiritually thunderous
our bodies and souls
know no interruption
the explosion will create a new path
a new way of being
a new horizon that only our eyes
are capable of seeing

(Jewel #555)
am I playing with fire
am I bound to get burned
am I a fool for thinking
that your equations can be learned
I thought I was up for the challenge
I thought I was the last brave man
I should have paid more attention
to all the ashes clutched in your hands

The Book of Born Free - Volume One

(Jewel #556)
in the 69 weeks
since we've been hitting the sheets
I've been a Priest, an ancient beast
and the crooked police
a doctor, a mugger
and even your step-brother
we do it all
when we're under the covers

(Jewel #557)
in the 69 weeks
since that first blind dinner
you've been a stripper, a gold digger
and a ruthless killer
a prostitute, a substitute
and my wife's best friend
I love that our strangeness
has no end

(Jewel #558)
I went for a walk with my dreams
and my brand-new notebook
I came across you naked and free
floating in the local brook
you swam and smiled
undeterred by the sad affairs of the day
and once you invited me in to play
all my worldly concerns floated away

The Book of Born Free - Volume One

(Jewel #559)
at this altitude
all we see is endless tranquility
no hypocritical cadences
or feelings of inadequacy
things appear magically
if we just believe they will
God brought us here
because our destiny must be fulfilled

(Jewel #560)
our love isn't for the comfortable
or the all-knowing
our love isn't for the big talker
or the never going
our love is for the weirdo's
and the unsung heroes
our love is for the outcasts
and those trapped in limbo

The Book of Born Free - Volume One

(Jewel #561)
our words are like Prometheus
stealing fire from Mt. Olympus
the power of our lyrical lust
makes me want to shout and bust
I can feel myself melting
into rivers of golden cosmic dust
it's going to take a minute
to adjust to this level of trust

(Jewel #562)
you've unzipped the sky
and let the light pour
I've never been this close
to rapture's front door
I've been in the ballpark
I've been on the field
I've made love to rumors
but nothing has been this real

(Jewel #563)
our love doesn't wear any makeup
or have any fancy clothes
our love doesn't go
where the brainwashed tend to go
we've charted a new path
across our vast inner planetary space
we walk hand in hand
under the approving smile on God's face

The Book of Born Free - Volume One

(Jewel #564)
thank you for killing the old me
thank you for setting me free
thank you for showing me
that I was my worst enemy
thank you for rebuilding me
thank you for making me a better man
thank you for reminding me
that God wants me to do the best I can

(Jewel #565)
as our bodies move
in perfect tandem
nothing we do or experience
will be random
nothing we say or encounter
will be a coincidence
everything that occurs
is because of His providence

The Book of Born Free - Volume One

(Jewel #566)
I love washing your body down
when we're dancing in the shower
I love slowly shaving around
your delicate African flower
I love rubbing warm coconut oil
on you from head to toe
I love looking into your brown eyes
and knowing exactly where to go

(Jewel #567)
our thoughts fly from treetop to mountaintop
from galaxy to galaxy
our alchemy
is our amnesty
our honesty
provides the perfect lubrication
for us to slide right into the center
of our own re-creation

(Jewel #568)
we have no room in our home
for a comfort zone
everything that we own amplifies
our passionate moans and groans
we've sacrificed our bodies, our spirits
our blood, our bones
to blast us past the outer realms
of the unaccepted and unknown

The Book of Born Free - Volume One

(Jewel #569)
we've both been hurt
we've both been discarded
we've both been abandoned
we've both been guarded
we've both been hoisted up on the rack
and beaten with the devil's lash
but we both showed the world
that you can survive your dark past

(Jewel #570)
we belong to each other
The Most High made the deal
Ezekiel saw us shining inside
the wheel within the wheel
Daniel saw us having a child
in his dreams and visions
and Yeshua gave us his blessing
as He set out on His father's mission

The Book of Born Free - Volume One

(Jewel #571)
cut deep into my skin
with your weapon of choice
break open my heart
with the sound of your voice
I'll use my tongue to write my vows
across your inner thigh
once we rub our cum across our eyes
we'll never grow old and die

(Jewel #572)
I love all of you
your good and bad thoughts
your heart, stretch marks
and the way your nipples glow in the dark
I can't love in bits and pieces
small chunks and fractions
I am all into the end
everything else is an unworthy distraction

(Jewel #573)
I don't care who came before me
I want to know everything
I want to hear about every deep love
and casual fling
no judgment, no punishment
no rejection
and if you don't believe my words
just feel my erection

The Book of Born Free - Volume One

(Jewel #574)
I want to know your every fantasy
even the ones that exclude me
I want to know what makes you
truly insatiable and hungry
do you desire more men, women
or more of everything
I want to know what truly
makes your passions sing

(Jewel #575)
safe sex, rough sex, consensual sex
we love sex
oral sex, anal sex, group sex
we love sex
loving sex, angry sex, make up sex
we love sex
phone sex, experimental sex, Tantric sex
we love sex

The Book of Born Free - Volume One

(Jewel #576)
I love all your desserts
your dark chocolate cake and sweet creampies
organic peach cobbler
with the hidden custard surprise
I love your caramel swirl
your deep-dish cookie bowl
everything that comes out of your oven
keeps me under your control

(Jewel #577)
turn on the webcam
let's invite them into our world
let's give them a small glimpse
of what makes our fingers and toes curl
open the chat box
let's give them a little tease
let's bring this entire internet
down on its knees

(Jewel #578)
this morning I watched some B.A.B.W.
last night P.A.W.G.
I dreamed about some B.D.S.M.
and masturbated to some E.G.N.D.
said yes to D.P.
with a stunning brown MILF
got some much needed XOXO
in a Jacuzzi of black milk

The Book of Born Free - Volume One

(Jewel #579)
some have big asses, big dicks
others have little asses, little dicks
flat stomachs, big tits
love handles, small lips
no matter what you've been given
be grateful and use them with vigor
happiness isn't guaranteed
if you were smaller or bigger

(Jewel #580)
don't look for the fountain of youth
in a procedure or jar
don't look for the love of your life
at a strip club or bar
the key to great parenting can't be downloaded
on your Kindle or Nook
all the answers are available
it just depends on where you look

The Book of Born Free - Volume One

(Jewel #581)
I love a woman
who reads and writes
in vibrant colors
and steely black and white
in shades of gray
and mixtures unknown
a woman like that
I long to call my own

(Jewel #582)
when you buy a new book
you make our relationship stronger
it makes our conversations juicier
and last much longer
reading to me in bed
takes our foreplay up to a whole other level
and confirms that we've found
something genuine and special

(Jewel #583)
what happens in our bedroom
is based on our life everywhere else
nothing is real
if real love isn't felt
you can have a random hit and run
that feels like the best
but if there's no real love
you just settled for infinitely less

The Book of Born Free - Volume One

(Jewel #584)
while you're in the next room
trying to think like a man
please don't turn into the kind of man
that you can't stand
cuz if your goal is to turn male stupidity
into female ignorance
you're about to think the next generation
right out of existence

(Jewel #585)
men aren't the only dogs
a lot of women walk off the leash
both our grasps
have exceeded our reach
don't get things twisted
we ALL need spiritual and sexual evolution
being honest with ourselves
is the first step towards a real solution

The Book of Born Free - Volume One

(Jewel #586)
fifty shades of Gray
is child's play
we tasted 69 colors
the other day
our erotic display
is an exquisite buffet
of culinary delights
and wicked foreplay

(Jewel #587)
legs over your head
arms around my neck
since we started with love and respect
we'll reach God's apex
with each stroke I can feel
your wet muscles tighten
at first, we were frightened
but now we're completely enlightened

(Jewel #588)
I love erotic stories
I love extra kink
I love warm massage oil
I love going over the brink
I love soft hands
I love pretty toes
I love ripping your ass
right out of your fuckin' clothes

The Book of Born Free - Volume One

(Jewel #589)
I have a vicious foot fetish
and I won't let it go
I love your soft bare feet
in and out of 5-inch stilettos
I love them in my mouth
I love their size and smell
I love them covered in chocolate
cum, and sticky caramel

(Jewel #590)
the only rival to being inside you
is lying beside you
basking in the luxurious dew
of your dark harmonious hue
the energy that radiates
defies all human logic
your eyes are hypnotic
and your pussy is pure cosmic chocolate

The Book of Born Free - Volume One

(Jewel #591)
our sex is condemned in public
but lusted for in private
the wingless secretly desire
to fly to our higher climate
they quietly get excited
because we're doing what they're afraid to do
they could enjoy this glory
if they only had the heart to

(Jewel #592)
our love was not born
on a butcher's block
Wonder and Bach
have written about our stock
we live inside the honeycomb
and vacation in the eyes of sunflowers
open the Book of Hours
to read our message to all the doubters

(Jewel #593)
our contract
isn't written on paper
it's written
in our very nature
this isn't a movie to us
this isn't a popular whim
we were driven to this beautiful place
by the force of God within

The Book of Born Free - Volume One

(Jewel #594)
I love being your sweet perversion
your twisted little jewel
your fantasy
and your obedient little fool
I jump through your hoops
I roll and bend over
I'll go higher or lower
you're the soul controller

(Jewel #595)
I don't need virginity
I need integrity
I don't need perfection
I need honesty
I don't need your money
I need sincerity
I don't need the world
I need loyalty

The Book of Born Free - Volume One

(Jewel #596)
PRINCE IS ALIVE
I can still feel his beating heart
legend says he fell asleep
somewhere inside the womb of **Paisley Park**
I believe he's taking a nap
this is just a musical interlude
until his glorious return
we'll continue his erotically sacred mood

(Jewel #597)
I like to dominate
and be dominated
I like to be righteously abused
and lovingly elevated
I like to feed as well as being fed
when in bed
I like to lead as well as being led
when out of bed

(Jewel #598)
you don't have to hide
your vibrator from me
you don't have to hide
your bi and lesbian porn from me
let's incorporate it all
in our daily and nightly sessions
honest expression
destroys dissatisfaction and deception

The Book of Born Free - Volume One

(Jewel #599)
your body beckoned me
across the starry chasm
your spirit guided me
beyond mediocre enthusiasm
your voice sang to me
in ancient harmonic waves
your love lifted me
out of my deep eremitic grave

(Jewel #600)
I won't let them rape you
I won't let them debase you
I won't let them disgrace you
I won't let them mis-educate you
I put my life on my word
and my word in God's unfailing hands
if they try to hurt you
I will kill them right where they stand

The Book of Born Free - Volume One

(Jewel #601)
our love is not based
on material possession
nor is it based on
carnal suggestions
it's rooted in the same
universal watery bliss
that causes all life
to vibrate and exist

(Jewel #602)
I don't want you prone
I don't want you incapacitated
I don't want you fucked up
I don't want you frustrated
I want you bright eyed and aware
I want you to see everything
I want you to confirm
that I've earned my wedding ring

(Jewel #603)
pillow fights
game nights
flying kites
ancient rites
in our prime
dope rhymes
mountain climbs
I would choose us a million times

The Book of Born Free - Volume One

(Jewel #604)
Prince left us clues
on how to save **Planet Earth**
he said, look inside the **Loutsflow3r**
to begin your search
if we enter as God's pilgrims
and make love in the crystal pavilion
he said, we'll give birth
to millions of beautiful **Rainbow Children**

(Jewel #605)
I love that we're still dating
9 years after we said I do
it's one of the strongest reasons
that we've never regretted saying I do
we continue to court and play
like we did in the honeymoon phase
I see fresh life inside your gaze
we show no signs of malaise

The Book of Born Free - Volume One

When the old spirits come

when the old spirits come
we will offer them the treasures of our lives
when the old spirits come
we can shed the skin of our earthly disguise
everlasting life awaits us
if we pay attention to the time
this old world is coming to an end
we can't afford to misread the signs
from our bedroom window
I can feel the darkness racing across the skies
I can see the decaying spiders
trapped inside the webs of their own lies
the compromised
praying for each other's demise
they sought out Satan as an ally
and helped give rise to his enterprise
they bought what was advertised
closed their ears to their children's cries
but those who demonize and colonize
will surely come up short and horribly die
I know that when the final judgment is done
our love will be alive and well
because the soul we were given at birth
we never tried to abuse or sell
so when the old spirits come
we will begin a new spiritual journey
when the old spirits come
we will fly above eternity
we don't need to packs any bags
all we need is a love that's one
and I know we'll be ready
when the old spirits come

Born Free #therealbornfree

The Book of Born Free - Volume One

(Jewel #606)
I don't acquiesce because
of what some silly gender war mandated
I submit, because you choose God
over what His creation created
you choose the light of the sky
over the glittery corporate lie
and those choices are why
I hold you up so high

(Jewel #607)
the darkness has departed our home
we're safe for now
we've burned our old clothes
and torn down all man-made sacred cows
our food is kosher
our speech is Halal
our protection comes from
what we've disavowed

(Jewel #608)
stand on the roof with me
a few new stars have been born
the air is filled with sweet lavender
and the current is gentle and warm
let's stand naked on the ledge
right on the edge where everyone can see
that true love doesn't need anything
but honesty and loyalty

The Book of Born Free - Volume One

(Jewel #609)
this world is trying to make us
small and minuscule
insecure
and the object of hateful ridicule
they're trying to keep us distracted
with scandalous empires
so we'll walk into the quagmire
and confuse Heaven with hellfire

(Jewel #610)
we weren't born to be watchers
or sideline romantics
watered down wicks
playing erotic games of avoidance and semantics
our hearts connection was the start
of our body's engagement in the war
God and gun are the only things
keeping them coming through the door

The Book of Born Free - Volume One

(Jewel #611)
gregarious to a fault
your manner is enchanting
your curves are haunting
they always leave me wanting
confronting this desire
wasn't an easy task
but your honest inspection
forced me to leave my past in the past

(Jewel #612)
fuck this digital disaster
romantic slave masters
they can't distract us
from God's royal rapture
they're not plugged in
so that can't feel this wild surge
our legacy was confirmed
the moment our loves light emerged

(Jewel #613)
the confederates and counterfeits
consort amongst the innocent
ply them with compliments
to undermine the penitent
but our love is resilient
and forcefully persistent
we shine with godly brilliance
and incinerate the ignorant

The Book of Born Free - Volume One

(Jewel #614)
I lost my job
and you still never doubted me
I revealed my fears
and you never abandoned me
I shed cold tears
and you continued to embrace me
I showed you my broken trust
and you kept on loving me

(Jewel #615)
I must do more than vainly exclaim
my love to the heavens
I must do more than just warm my hands
by the fire of your presence
love is doing the work
love is the soul of action
I must not get caught up on the lower ladder
of causal base passion

The Book of Born Free - Volume One

(Jewel #616)
if you love her
why are you looking over her shoulder
the payment for secret summer promises
is something much colder
if you love him
why advance your co-workers glance
the payment for sweet snowflake kisses
is a deadly avalanche

(Jewel #617)
don't let the sexy barking of wild dogs
lure you over the fence
remember your vows
think of the consequence
these stray dogs bite
they even ravage the bones
remember your family, your home
and remember the fall of Rome

(Jewel #618)
no relationship is without contention
love is born on turbulent seas
a wintery cool breeze
knocks many of the trapeze
lovers disagree
this is a lover's reality
but if you stay faithful to the decree
you'll get the Kingdom's keys

The Book of Born Free - Volume One

(Jewel #619)
love at first sight
is only proven with time
some passionate wildfires
burn out well before their prime
take it day by day
don't try to leap too far ahead
or you might find a casket
lying patiently under your new lover's bed

(Jewel #620)
I've seen a lot of good families
fall prey to misinterpretations
they let outside people
cause their separation
they treated the ghetto gossip
like it was supreme revelation
and the death blow came
when they stopped all direct communication

The Book of Born Free - Volume One

(Jewel #621)
I wish I could tell you
that love was an easy ride
I wish I could say that you and your love
will never collide
truth be told
love runs hot and cold
but when you get it right
it's a beautiful sight to behold

(Jewel #622)
if you love me then tell me
don't wait until I notice the signs
the only thing more precious than love
is time
there are no perfect moments, perfect jobs
or perfect locations
courage is all you need
to make this a divine consecration

(Jewel #623)
stop lying to yourself
about your true feelings
stop lying to your partner
about your true dealings
stop leaving the room
every time you answer your phone
stop everything that will cause
the destruction of your home

The Book of Born Free - Volume One

(Jewel #624)
there are a million different kinds
of love affairs
some fit inside circles
others inside squares
some lean towards the sun
others favor the moon
but without truth and compromise
they all meet their doom

(Jewel #625)
you are my beloved
my one true beloved
the devil covets
because of what God has led us to discover
what we call love
is really the path back to His grace
God has given us His permission
to climb His never-ending staircase

The Book of Born Free - Volume One

(Jewel #626)
something magical
swirls around your eyes
dreams and destiny fly by
and collide
they make love, have children
and happily, die
they leave footprints for us to follow
across the ambient sky

(Jewel #627)
I wrote this for you
I removed my armor and mesh
I striped down naked
and pealed back my flesh
I've laid everything bare
now you know what I know
I pray that my humble offering
helps us get closer and grow

(Jewel #628)
I would choose you today
just like I chose you back then
you are the love of my life
and my dearest friend
the genuine simplicity of what we have
holds everything together
and the bottom line is
we make each other stronger and better

The Book of Born Free - Volume One

(Jewel #629)
I pledge to be more than my words
more than my quotes
more than my posts
more than a ghost
more than a sweet promise
more than raw potential
telling you is wonderful
but showing you is essential

(Jewel #630)
prayers do get answered
messages do get through
make sure you're open and available
when they come back to you
when God sends you the love
you've been praying for
make sure that you've taken
the top and bottom locks off the doors

The Book of Born Free - Volume One

THANK YOU BELOVED,

let's continue to talk

and LOVE EACH OTHER!!!

The Book of Born Free - Volume One

whoever uncorks this message
don't delay in its delivery
learn from history
LOVE is liberty
it's not a mystery
deadly greed consumed us in our wrath
don't bring back the worse of us
follow a new and loving path

Born Free #therealbornfree

The Book of Born Free - Volume One

BONUS JEWELS

The Book of Born Free - Volume One

(Bonus Jewel #ONE)
Trump tweets about debt
not the destruction in Puerto Rico
he has the mind of a mosquito
racist orange Cheeto in a tuxedo
launch the torpedoes
destroy that massive ego
bury this idiotic sideshow
beneath one of his bankrupt casinos

(Bonus Jewel #TWO)
Trump didn't go crazy
Trump isn't off the rails
Trump didn't go rouge
Trump isn't sniffing chemtrails
what Trump showed yesterday
is what he was on his first birthday
you can't vote or pray
white supremacy away

(Bonus Jewel #THREE)
fuck Donald Trump from all sides
fuck all his allies
his kids, his bride
and anyone else who subscribes to his lies
no moral equivalency
with the white supremacy trying kill me
if that's what you see
you're my open enemy

The Book of Born Free - Volume One

(Bonus Jewel #FOUR)
white supremacy isn't a gang of idiots
in Charlottesville spewing hate
its deeper expression
is right on your dinner plate
white supremacy is more
than the preservation of confederate folklore
it's manifested in who controls
black life from seashore to seashore

(Bonus Jewel #FIVE)
black nationalism is nothing like
white nationalism
the former is human pragmatism
the latter is inhumane despotism
we're not trying to eliminate
we're trying to get our lives straight
counteract the hate and elevate
our children's economic and social state

The Book of Born Free - Volume One

(Bonus Jewel #SIX)
a van plows into people in Barcelona
its labeled terrorism in seconds
a car plows into people in Charlottesville
Trump ignores the question
Terrorism is terrorism
the same vile organism
separating them
shows your ignorance and barbarism

(Bonus Jewel #SEVEN)
where the fuck is all these
hardcore black gangs
the ones who love to take aim
and blow out black brains
the bloods and crips should be the first to enlist
against these terrorists
if you're not confronting this
you're just a little bitch talking dumb shit

(Bonus Jewel #EIGHT)
these devils march without hoods
cuz they're not afraid of us
they know which direction
our guns bust
and it's not at them
or their wicked kith or kin
black men are still shamefully
killing other black women and men

The Book of Born Free - Volume One

(Bonus Jewel #NINE)
1,503 symbols
of confederate devils memorialized
no matter how much their criticized
they were all authorized
franchised, advertised
and normalized
taking them down
is allowing them to hide their lies

(Bonus Jewel #TEN)
don't focus on the statues
it's the racist's laws and statutes
control of trade routes
that put our youth in prison suits
don't sip the soup
or follow pedophile piper's flutes
be astute
don't get led on a fruitless pursuit

The Book of Born Free - Volume One

(Bonus Jewel #ELEVEN)
Trump didn't lose his moral authority
that bitch never had it
hiding his abusive habits
is closing America's casket
he wants us to see nice Nazis
and respectable racists
FUCK this sadist
I'm all out of patience

(Bonus Jewel #TWELVE)
don't get caught up in political conventions
devilish dimensions
red and blue pretensions
they all have bad intentions
NO exceptions
research every election
if you can't see the connections
you're living proof of inception

(Bonus Jewel #THIRTEEN)
don't be content to be a witness
a faded poster
unconscious sober voter
a foul odor promoter
we can't keep our composure
in neutral revving the motor
hate-hates exposure
don't die with your gun unloaded in the holster

The Book of Born Free - Volume One

(Bonus Jewel #FOURTEEN)
the media's rhetoric is tryin'
to humanize this white terrorist
praying this sick degenerate
had some kind of therapist
some kind of prescriptions
some crazy past twist
so, they can keep Stephen Paddock
off the list with the other global terrorists

(Bonus Jewel #FIFTEEN)
how can Vegas be the worst
what about Tulsa in 1921
with torch and gun
white mobs tried to kill everyone
300 black lives died
6,000 arrested for defending the rest
I WILL NEVER FORGET
WE WILL NEVER FORGET!

The Book of Born Free - Volume One

(Bonus Jewel #SIXTEEN)
no matter why massacres happen
no matter the root cause
America must pause
rethink its society and gun laws
and since black-death
doesn't move the discussion
maybe all this white blood gushin'
will motivate them to do something

(Bonus Jewel #SEVENTEEN)
the fact that Weinstein thinks his assaults
were consensual is twisted
it's like Thomas Jefferson
calling Sally Heming's his mistress
Sally was a rape victim
Jefferson was her enslaver and rapist
Harvey and Thomas are a part
of the same vile matrix

(Bonus Jewel #EIGHTEEN)
it pains me through and through
that so many women are #MeToo
every race, every place
every economic state is #MeToo
as men we must do more
than verbally have our women's backs
we must face the sad fact
that we are the source of these attacks

The Book of Born Free - Volume One

(Bonus Jewel #NINETEEN)
sexual predators
don't have a sexual addiction
this sick depiction
is a horribly false description
only a monster would confuse
sexual abuse with consent
I lament cuz this is the same place
that made a predator the president

(Bonus Jewel #TWENTY)
every woman crushed to the earth
shall rise like the phoenix
in all arenas
we'll expel these jackals and hyenas
every woman hurt, bullied
abused and killed
will be avenged until
the final truth is revealed

The Book of Born Free - Volume One

(Bonus Jewel #TWENTY-ONE)
who cares what you believe
if you won't clean up your own block!
who cares what you believe
if you won't invest in your own stocks!
who cares what you believe
if you're not building an actual building!
who cares what you believe
if you won't empower your own children!

(Bonus Jewel #TWENTY-TWO)
the U.S. government
can't get out of this unscathed
depraved; they're at the root
of Africans in Libya being enslaved
we all know the reason
they helped destabilize the region
no more false teachin'
America set loose these slave trader demons

(Bonus Jewel #TWENTY-THREE)
the glitch is the Matrix
we're caught in a loop
we suffer cuz we're not
economically president proof
independent, self sufficient
with freedom's clear vision
words without conviction
are fictitious positions

The Book of Born Free - Volume One

(Bonus Jewel #TWENTY-FOUR)
if we make black nationalism
our collective social theory
our great-great grandchildren
will breathe and sleep easy
if we make empty rhetoric and death
the way we relate to each other
our great-great grandchildren
will die from thirst and hunger

(Bonus Jewel #TWENTY-FIVE)
fuck a trickle-down theory
Yurugu economics
if you believe a demonic promise
you're an enemy of the prophet's
we must sell our own products
increase our own profits
a victory is not a victory
if it's only symbolic

The Book of Born Free - Volume One

(Bonus Jewel #TWENTY-SIX)
maybe we needed this pressure
to feel the devil's heat
to be seasoned meat
fattened up for the feast
we only focus our steps
when we're under constant threat
why do we only fight for love and self respect
at the precipice of death?

(Bonus Jewel #TWENTY-SEVEN)
let's not be spectators
and nail bitters
passive riders
and distracted writers
See somethin', say somethin'
feel somethin', do somethin'
stop frontin', we have the power
to stop the apocalypse comin!

The Book of Born Free - Volume One

About the Author

Carl Born Free Wharton was born and primarily raised in Philadelphia, Pennsylvania. He grew up in West Philly in a so-called "middle class" area called Wynnefield. He spent some of his formative years down "The Bottom" at his Beloved Grandmother's (Pauline Ramsey) house on 38th & Poplar. The harsh dichotomies and undeniable similarities between these two neighborhoods taught and showed him graphically the range of black life during the 70's, 80's and 90's. He knew a life before crack and one after crack, and that created inside his soul a relentless conscious perspective that was born to stand on the frontlines of the struggle for freedom, justice, and equality.

The fabric of his community was forever changed during the governmental assault of guns, drugs, and mis-education. Born was determined to find out who was responsible for these horrendous crimes. Since Born was raised and came of age during Hip Hop's Cultural Revolution, he understands the supreme importance of the written and spoken word.

The Book of Born Free - Volume One

His love of reading and exploring the great pantheon of black writers and other great literary figures set him on the path of becoming a deep thinker and lifelong scribe. Born Free wants to communicate and connect with the reader's heart by invoking raw emotions and holding up a mirror, so we can examine ourselves and the world around us.

Love is the connective tissue that unites everything that he does and writes about. Love is the fire that burns brilliantly in his heart. Born lives to write and build on a variety of classical and contemporary ideas and thoughts but his greatest desire is to compel the reader to get the hell up and confront this life right here and right now! He wants us to activate our activism and use our God given talents to bring light to a world increasingly becoming dark.

The Book of Born Free - Volume One

Follow Born Free
on all social media platforms
#therealbornfree

Contact @ therealbornfree@gmail.com

Copyright © 2017
Conscious Commentary Publishing
LLC

The Book of Born Free - Volume One

The Book of Born Free - Volume One

FIGHT BACK!!!!!!!!!!

LOVE BACK!!!!!!!!!!!!

FIGHT BACK!!!!!!!!!!

LOVE BACK!!!!!!!!!!!!

FIGHT BACK!!!!!!!!!!

LOVE BACK!!!!!!!!!!!!

FIGHT BACK!!!!!!!!!!

LOVE BACK!!!!!!!!!!!!

FIGHT BACK!!!!!!!!!!

LOVE BACK!!!!!!!!!!!!

FIGHT BACK!!!!!!!!!!

LOVE BACK!!!!!!!!!!!!

FIGHT BACK!!!!!!!!!!

LOVE BACK!!!!!!!!!!!!

The Book of Born Free - Volume One

The Book of Born Free - Volume One

www.ingramcontent.com/pod-product-compliance
Lightning Source LLC
Chambersburg PA
CBHW032039090426
42744CB00004B/65